Coherence, Truth and Testimony

Edited by

Ulrich Gähde
University of Hamburg,
Hamburg, Germany

and

Stephan Hartmann
London School of Economics and Political Science,
London, UK and
University of Konstanz,
Konstanz, Germany

Reprinted from *Erkenntnis* 63 No. 3 (2005)

 Springer

A C.I.P. Catalogue record for this book is available from the Library of Congress.

ISBN 1-4020-4426-7

Published by Springer,
P.O. Box 17, 3300 AA Dordrecht, The Netherlands.

Sold and distributed in North, Central and South America
by Springer,
101 Philip Drive, Norwell, MA 02061, U.S.A

In all other countries, sold and distributed
by Springer,
P.O. Box 17, 3300 AA Dordrecht, The Netherlands.

Printed on acid-free paper

Printed in the Netherlands

Table of Contents

Erkenntnis (2005) 63:293–294
DOI 10.1007/s10670-005-4006-0

EDITORIAL

This special issue delves into the epistemological concept of coherence with a collection of seven papers dedicated to the topic. One important topic addressed is an explication of coherence. Authors in this collection demonstrate the breadth of strategies applied in response to the challenge by considering both explanatory and probabilistic accounts. In addition to offering a definition of the concept, many of these authors also take up the challenging and controversial task of measuring the coherence of an information set. Other papers in this collection explore the epistemological and metaphysical implications of the notion of coherence. In this line of investigation, many authors consider the relationship between coherence and truth. Is coherence truth conducive, and if yes, under which conditions? The answer to this question has important implications for the coherence theory of justification. A related issue taken up in this special issue is the connection between coherence and testimony. Are we justified in believing coherent reports by independent, though only partially reliable witnesses more than a single report? If yes, under which conditions does this claim hold true? In addition to its philosophical importance, this question is also of practical interest, as court cases demonstrate.

This collection grew out of a workshop on *Coherence* at the conference GAP.5 in Bielefeld, Germany (September 26–27, 2003). We acknowledge the generous support of the workshop by the *Gesellschaft für analytische Philosophie e.V.* and thank the organizers of the conference for their support. The papers by Luc Bovens & Stephan Hartmann, Erik Olsson and Tomoji Shogenji were presented at this workshop. Additionally, the articles by David Glass, Keith Lehrer, Mark Siebel and Paul Thagard were commissioned. We thank all authors and referees for their work. A special thanks is due to Hans Rott, the editor-in-chief of *Erkenntnis*, for his support of this special issue on *Coherence, Truth and Testimony.*

Ulrich Gähde
Philosophisches Seminar
Universität Hamburg
Von-Melle-Park 6
D-20146 Hamburg
Germany
E-mail: ulrich.gaehde@uni-hamburg.de

Stephan Hartmann
Department of Philosophy
Logic and Scientific Method
London School of Economics and Political Science
Houghton Street, London WC2A 2AE
UK

and

Philosophy, Probability and Modeling Research Group,
Center for Junior Research Fellows
University of Konstanz
M 682D-78457 Konstanz
Germany

Erkenntnis (2005) 63:295–316
DOI 10.1007/s10670-005-4004-2

PAUL THAGARD

TESTIMONY, CREDIBILITY, AND EXPLANATORY COHERENCE

ABSTRACT. This paper develops a descriptive and normative account of how people respond to testimony. It postulates a *default pathway* in which people more or less automatically respond to a claim by accepting it, as long as the claim made is consistent with their beliefs and the source is credible. Otherwise, people enter a *reflective pathway* in which they evaluate the claim based on its explanatory coherence with everything else they believe. Computer simulations show how explanatory coherence can be maximized in real-life cases, taking into account all the relevant evidence including the credibility of whoever is making a claim. The explanatory-coherence account is more plausible both descriptively and normatively than a Bayesian account.

1. INTRODUCTION

When someone tells you something, should you believe it? This problem is ubiquitous in law, business, science, and everyday life. It arises in law when jurors and judges have to decide whether to believe the testimony of a witness. It arises in business when buyers, sellers, and others make claims that may be dubious. The problem arises in science when researchers report experimental results that may be true but alternatively might be the result of fraud or incompetence. Finally, in everyday life we usually accept the statements of friends, colleagues, and acquaintances, but we sometimes need to doubt their veracity. All of these are cases of testimony, where people usually accept but sometimes reject what is told to them.

Many philosophers have noted the heavy dependence of human knowledge on testimony (see, for example, Coady, 1992; Audi, 1997; Lipton, 1998). But there is currently no general theory of how people do and how people should respond to testimony. This paper develops a framework for both a descriptive, psychological theory of testimony response and a prescriptive, philosophical theory of how people can best respond to testimony. In the spirit of naturalistic epistemology, the prescriptive theory is intimately related to the

[3]

descriptive theory, in that it describes how people evaluate testimony
when they are doing it best.

Section 2 provides a general account of how people respond to
testimony. It postulates a *default pathway* in which people more or
less automatically respond to a claim by accepting it, as long as the
claim made is consistent with their beliefs and the source is credible.
When these two conditions are violated, however, people enter a
reflective pathway in which they evaluate the claim based on its
explanatory coherence with everything else they believe. People
usually do and always should accept a claim if and only if accepting
the claim maximizes explanatory coherence. A person's making a
claim can always be explained in different ways, for example by the
hypotheses that the person really believes the claim and has evidence
for it, or alternatively by the hypotheses that the person does not
believe the claim and is trying to deceive the listeners. Listeners need
to decide which of the competing explanations is most coherent with
all the evidence, including what is known about the credibility of the
person making the claim. You should believe a claim made by a
person if its truth is part of the best explanation of all the evidence
relevant to the claim (Lipton, 1998).

Sections 3–5 develop in detail the explanatory-coherence theory of
reflective response to testimony. I show how it applies to real-life
cases, including a business case involving an Internet bulletin board
and a legal case involving a police officer's testimony. Computer
simulations show how explanatory coherence can be maximized in
these and other cases, taking into account all the relevant evidence
including the credibility of whoever is making a claim. Section 6
provides an extended discussion of credibility, arguing that it is different from reliability construed as a conditional probability. Section
7 contrasts the explanatory-coherence theory of testimony with the
Bayesian theory that says that testimony should be evaluated using
the resources of probability theory. After describing a Bayesian
simulation of the business case previously discussed, I argue that the
explanatory-coherence account is more plausible both descriptively
and normatively than the Bayesian account.

2. THE PROCESS OF RESPONDING TO TESTIMONY

In the course of a day, people hear or read hundreds of statements
from other people and various media, including television, radio,
newspapers and the Internet. I believe most of what I hear without

much reflection, for example the TV's weather forecast, the newspaper's report of the sports scores, and my sons' descriptions of their activities at school. Occasionally, however, I encounter a claim that is dubious, for example when my son says that he does not have much homework when I know he has a big assignment due. At that point I start to wonder about why he might be saying that he does not have much homework, for example because he wants to play video games instead. In addition, when I encounter a report from a source that I know to be unreliable such as a supermarket tabloid, I do not automatically accept the claim.

A general theory of testimony has to be able to explain both how testimony is usually accepted automatically but also how it sometimes provokes extensive reflection about the claim being made and the claimant who is making it. Figure 1 is a proposal about the psychological processes that arise in people responding to testimonial claims. It suggests that when people encounter a claim made by a person or other source there is an unconscious assessment of the claim and its source. Usually, the claim passes these two tests and is accepted without reflection. The top part of Figure 1 illustrates the *default pathway* in which claims are quickly accepted. However, if the claim is inconsistent with what the person believes or if the source is known to lack credibility then reflection is triggered. The result, shown in the bottom part of Figure 1, is a much more extended process of assessing the explanatory coherence of the claim, which is discussed in Section 4. I call this bottom part the *reflective pathway*. The hypothesis that people tend to accept testimony by default has previously been suggested by Burge (1993), Diller (2000), Fricker (1994), Lipton (1998), and Reid (1970). Figure 1 goes beyond these

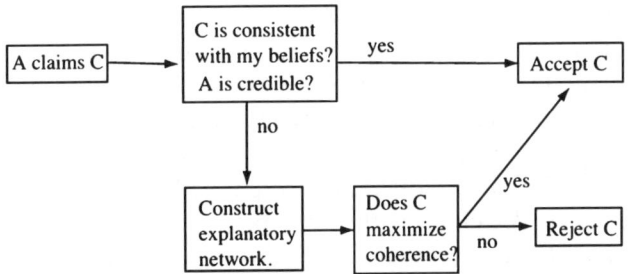

Figure 1. Dual-pathway model of response to testimony in which a person or other source A makes a statement C. The top part is the default pathway, and the bottom part is the reflective pathway.

suggestions in showing the relation between the default and reflective pathways.

From a descriptive, psychological perspective, Figure 1 is over-simplified in several respects. It omits a prior process by which an utterance is interpreted as a claim rather than a different kind of utterance such as a joke. If a person utters a sentence while winking or giggling, you will infer that the sentence is intended to make you laugh, not as a claim that you are supposed to believe. Similarly, the overall behavior and context of sources can itself raise questions about their credibility, for example if a person is making a claim while avoiding eye contact and sweating profusely. Hence the credibility check in the box in the top row of Figure 1 may include both general information about the source and particular, contextual information about it.

When you hear an utterance that is inconsistent with what you already believe, your response is usually emotional, ranging from mild surprise or puzzlement to stronger reactions such as annoyance or even anger. Prescriptively, it seems appropriate not to accept claims that are inconsistent with what you believe. But such claims should not be automatically rejected either, because there may be more evidence for the claim than for what you believe: the fact that a credible source states the claim is one such piece of evidence. So what you ought to do is to consider more thoroughly whether to accept or reject the claim, as shown in the reflective pathway of Figure 1.

Do people actually do this? I know of no experiments that show that people become reflective when a claim is made that is inconsistent with their beliefs, as opposed to simply rejecting the claim. There is, however, considerable evidence that people are often inclined not to accept claims that are incompatible with their personal goals (Kunda, 1990). For example, when coffee drinkers are given a mock newspaper article that links cancer with caffeine consumption, they are less inclined to believe the claim than people who do not drink coffee. This kind of motivated inference is not normatively appropriate, but the fact that it triggers a more reflective kind of inference makes it plausible that inconsistency would also have the same kind of effect. Descriptively, then we have four kinds of reflection triggers: lack of credibility of the source, non-credible behavior of the source, inconsistency of the claim with other beliefs, and incompatibility of the claim with the hearer's goals. Prescriptively, all of these seem like good grounds for additional, more reflective processing, except possibly for the last. I am not sure whether motivation should or should not be a reflective trigger. It might seem on the negative side that using practical concerns to trigger reflection would create a bias toward believing what you want to believe, because if you like a conclusion you will not query it. On the other hand, if motivation is excluded from the reflective pathway, as it should be, then it will not bias the evaluation of the explanatory coherence of claims, so that triggering reflection on the basis of motivation will not contribute to the acceptance of defective claims. Moreover, from the perspective of practical rationality, which directs us toward accomplishing our goals, it may be useful to challenge information that is incompatible with those goals.

Descriptively, the overall process depicted in Figure 1 appears accurate, in that people do not challenge most of the claims that they encounter every day. We can ask, however, whether the default pathway is prescriptively appropriate: perhaps it would be epistemologically better always to use the reflective pathway, for the sake of obtaining fewer false beliefs. According to a recent study, lies are frequent in everyday conversation; 60% of participants in an experiment lied during a 10-min conversation, and did so an average of almost three times (Feldman et al., 2002). Our epistemic goals, however, go beyond just avoiding false beliefs; we want also to have a large number of important and useful beliefs. If we tried to reflect about every one of the statements that we encounter, we would be greatly restricted in the number of beliefs we could acquire. Moreover, everyday life would become impractical, in that we would spend so much time reflecting that we would never have time to do anything. We would be like the psychiatrist in the joke who, after a friend greeted him with "Hi, how are you?" muttered: "I wonder what she meant by that?" So I conclude that dividing response to testimony into the dual pathways displayed in Figure 1 is prescriptively as well as descriptively appropriate.

Much more contentious is the nature of the reflective pathway in that figure. The rest of the paper will argue for an explanatory-coherence interpretation of reflective response to testimony. I return to the general question of the justification of beliefs based on testimony in the concluding Section 8.

3. CASE STUDY 1: AN INTERNET BULLETIN BOARD

I begin with a real case that shows the need to evaluate claims made by other people. I regularly follow an Internet bulletin board that discusses a small Canadian company, Oncolytics Biotech. This company is investigating the use of a naturally occurring virus, called the reovirus, to treat cancer. The reovirus has been amazingly successful in killing many kinds of cancer cells in test tubes and in mice. Moreover, a phase 1 clinical trial that was primarily aimed at testing for the safety of administering the reovirus to humans found evidence of viral activity affecting tumors in 12 of 18 patients treated. Additional trials are underway to determine the effectiveness of the reovirus treatment on patients with various forms brain cancer. For a description and analysis of the discovery that the reovirus is capable of killing cancer cells, see Thagard (2002).

The Oncolytics Biotech bulletin board can be found on the Web site, http://www.stockhouse.ca/. Almost every day there are dozens of messages posted anonymously by Stockhouse members with obscure names such as *Dave54*. Some regular participants are very enthusiastic about the prospects of the Oncolytics Biotech based on their expectations that the reovirus will prove to be a successful and lucrative therapy; the main enthusiasts include Bioeye, Blue"chip", PullDaTrigger, and Matdu1 (I am not making these names up). Other participants have been much more skeptical about the company's prospects, for example Dandak and BeammeupToddy. Many of the postings have little content, with pumpers saying that the stock will go up and dumpers saying that it will go down. But there have also been messages that are highly informative about the science behind the reovirus treatment of cancer and the commercial activities of the company that is developing it.

Suppose you read the messages posed on the Oncolytics Biotech board, perhaps because you are thinking of investing in the company or perhaps because you have an interest in new cancer treatments. The problem of testimony arises whenever a member makes a substantive claim: should you believe it or not? For example, if someone posts that some positive experimental results will be announced the next day, you need to decide whether the poster is sufficiently credible that you can believe what is claimed. I have found Bioeye to be one of the most consistently well informed and reliable contributors to the bulletin board, so when she makes statements I tend to believe them (one of the other members reported without response that Bioeye is female; most of the other posters seem to be male). On the other hand, the main dumpers such as Dandak and BeammeupToddy never seem to have much information to contribute, so I have found no reason to believe their claims that the company is worthless. I should note, however, that despite some good scientific results the company's stock price is much lower in 2004 than when it peaked in 2000.

The descriptive question, then, is: Why do I usually believe Bioeye's claims and dismiss Dandak's claims? The normative question is: Am I justified in believing Bioeye's claims and dismissing Dandak's? Notice that the problem of testimony is particularly acute in Internet bulletin boards and chat rooms because there is little information about the identity, background, and motivations of the anonymous participants. In contrast to legal witnesses, there is no way of determining the identity of the people posting messages and whether they are in a position to know what they claim is true. Nevertheless, it is sometimes possible to assess the believability of different claims, and the next section analyses this case in terms of explanatory coherence.

The analysis to come concerns the reflective pathway, but much of what I read on the bulletin board can be accepted via the more direct default pathway. If there are postings by Bioeye, Matdul, or Blue"chip", all of whom have established credibility from a history of good messages, then I accept their claims without much reflection as long as the posting is consistent with what I already believe. See Section 7 for a discussion of how to evaluate the credibility of various people.

4. TESTIMONY AND EXPLANATORY COHERENCE

When Bioeye, Dandak or other member makes a claim that triggers reflection, I need to ask why they are making the claim. The positive explanation in Bioeye's case is that she made the claim because she believed it, and she believed it because she was in a position to know that it was true. For example, she was the first to report in September, 2001, that the announcement of the results of the phase 1 clinical trial would be delayed beyond the time period that the company had previously specified. It therefore seems to me that she has some good contacts in the company that put her in a position to know what it is doing. Of course, I would be rather gullible if I did not take into account possible alternative explanations of why Bioeye is making the claim that she did. She may simply be mistaken, having gotten her information from an unreliable source. More seriously, she may be trying to trick the members of the board into buying or selling stock so that she can increase her own trading profits. What I need to do is to try to decide whether the best explanation of Bioeye's making the claim is that she believes it because it is true, or alternatively that she believes it even though it is false or that she knows it is false but wants to mislead people. Similarly, when I read Dandak's posts, which routinely predicted without much evidence the precipitous decline of the stock price for Oncolytics Biotech, I need to ask why he is making such claims. Because he does not seem to have any evidence for them, I tend to conclude that he is simply trying to depress the stock price, presumably because he has shorted the stock, i.e. borrowed shares to sell with the prospect of buying them back later at a much lower price.

The structure of the inferences to believe Bioeye and disbelieve Dandak can be analyzed using the theory of explanatory coherence and the computer model ECHO. They have already been applied to a great many examples inference in science, law, and everyday life (see for example Thagard, 1989, 1999, 2000). The theory of explanatory coherence consists of the following principles:

PRINCIPLE E1. SYMMETRY. Explanatory coherence is a symmetric relation, unlike, say, conditional probability. That is, two propositions p and q cohere with each other equally.

PRINCIPLE E2. EXPLANATION. (a) A hypothesis coheres with what it explains, which can either be evidence or another hypothesis; (b) hypotheses that together explain some other proposition cohere with each other; and (c) the more hypotheses it takes to explain something, the lower the degree of coherence.

PRINCIPLE E3. ANALOGY. Similar hypotheses that explain similar pieces of evidence cohere.

PRINCIPLE E4. DATA PRIORITY. Propositions that describe the results of observations have a degree of acceptability on their own.

PRINCIPLE E5. CONTRADICTION. Contradictory propositions are incoherent with each other.

PRINCIPLE E6. COMPETITION. If P and Q both explain a proposition, and if P and Q are not explanatorily connected, then P and Q are incoherent with each other. (P and Q are explanatorily connected if one explains the other or if together they explain something.)

PRINCIPLE E7. ACCEPTANCE. The acceptability of a proposition in a system of propositions depends on its coherence with them.

These principles do not fully specify how to determine coherence-based acceptance, but algorithms are available that can compute acceptance and rejection of propositions on the basis of coherence relations. The most psychologically natural algorithms use artificial neural networks that represent propositions by artificial neurons or *units* and represent coherence and incoherence relations by excitatory and inhibitory links between the units that represent the propositions. Acceptance or rejection of a proposition is represented by the degree of activation of the unit. The program ECHO spreads activation among all units in a network until some units are activated and others are inactivated, in a way that maximizes the coherence of all the propositions represented by the units. I will not present the technical details here, since they are available elsewhere (Thagard, 1999, 2000).

Appendix A list the input given to ECHO to simulate the evaluation of a claim by Bioeye that a clinical trial has been completed. The explanatory structure of the case is best grasped through Figure 2, which shows the relevant propositions and the coherence relations among them. The only piece of evidence in the network is that Bioeye says that the trial is done. The crucial question is why she says that. Figure 2 displays two possible explanations, one that she says it because she believes it, and the alternative that she says it because she is lying. That she is lying would be explained by her desire to manipulate the stock price. On the other side, there are two available explanations of why she believes that the trial is done: that she is mistaken as the result of some erroneous information or inference, and alternatively that she has good evidence that the trial is done. The top-level hypothesis that the trial really is done would be part of the explanation of why she has good evidence that the trial is done. All of these explanatory relations are represented in Figure 2 by solid thin lines. The contradictions in the explanatory network are represented in Figure 2 by dotted thick lines: the hypothesis that the

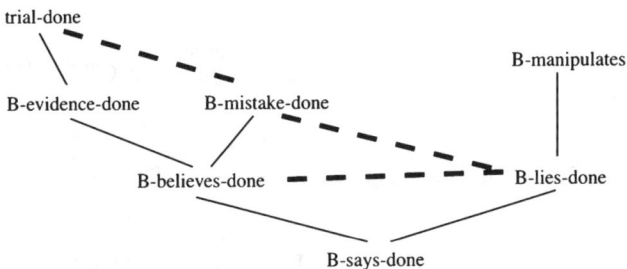

Figure 2. Explanatory coherence network of propositions determining whether to believe Bioeye. Solid lines indicate coherence relations, and dotted lines indicate incoherence relations. See Appendix A for the propositions.

trial is done contradicts both that Bioeye is mistaken and that the trial is done and that she is lying about whether it is done.

By itself, the network shown in Figure 2 is not sufficient to determine solidly which explanations are acceptable. In accord with explanatory coherence principle E4 (Data Priority), the unit representing *B-says-done* has an excitatory link with a special DATA unit that is always activated, so *B-says-done* is activated (in more complicated examples, however, data can be rejected, so explanatory coherence is not foundationalist). Running the network shown in Figure 2 leads to a weak conclusion that Bioeye is lying and that it is false that the trial is done. Activation spreads from *B-says-done* to *B-lies-done* and *B-believes-done*, which suppress each other's activation because of the inhibitory link between them, and then to all other hypotheses. Eventually, after dozens of iterations of spreading activation among units, the network settles (i.e. the activation of all units stabilizes) leaving *B-lies-done* with the slight advantage.

What is missing from the simulation shown in Figure 2 is a hypothesis about Bioeye's credibility. Anyone following the Oncolytics Biotech bulletin board regularly has experience of Bioeye making claims that are consistent with available scientific information and that usually turn out to be true. Thus a crucial part of the explanatory-coherence inference about whether to believe Bioeye requires some information about her credibility.

Figure 3 shows an expanded version of Figure 2 that shows how credibility fits into the explanatory-coherence account. If the unit representing the hypothesis that Bioeye is credible is supported by DATA, then it tends to become activated and thereby deactivates the hypotheses that Bioeye is mistaken or lying. The result is acceptance of the hypotheses that Bioeye has evidence that the trial is done and

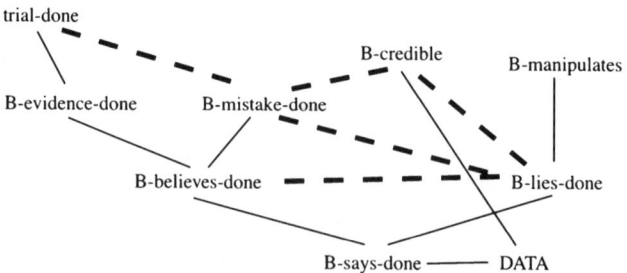

Figure 3. Explanatory coherence network of propositions determining whether to believe Bioeye, taking into account her credibility. Solid lines indicate coherence relations, and dotted lines indicate incoherence relations.

that the trial is in fact done. The hypothesis that Bioeye is credible is crucial to the overall assessment because it militates against the hypotheses that go against the hypothesis that she is telling the truth. Here the DATA unit does not represent any particular piece of information: it is merely a programming device for providing activation to units that represent propositions based on observational evidence, and the link with the unit representing B's credibility assumes that there is some such evidence that supports it.

Figure 3 is an advance on Figure 2 in that it takes credibility into account, but it does not say much about how credibility is determined, taking it simply as a kind of data. I will argue in Section 6, however, that inferences about credibility are more complex. First, however, I want to present another case study of inference in which testimony is rejected.

5. CASE STUDY 2: O. J. SIMPSON AND MARK FUHRMAN

To further illustrate how the evaluation of testimony can be based on explanatory coherence, consider the role of Detective Mark Fuhrman in the notorious trial of O. J. Simpson, who was accused of killing his wife. Fuhrman was one of the detectives who arrived at Simpson's house after the murder was reported, and he claimed to have found a bloody glove in Simpson's back yard. The glove belonged to Simpson and the blood matched that of the murdered wife, so this was a strong piece of evidence implicating Simpson. It seemed that the best explanation of the presence of the bloody glove in Simpson's yard was the hypothesis that he had murdered his wife.

At the trial, however, the defense succeed in raising major questions about Furhman's credibility (Schiller and Willwerth, 1997; Thagard, 2003). He denied being a racist and using the word "nigger", but evidence was found that he frequently used the word and even bragged about harassing black men accompanied by white women. Some members of the jury said afterwards that after the revelations about Fuhrman they could not take seriously anything he said. The structure of the explanatory-coherence inference about Fuhrman is shown in Figure 4. The hypothesis that the bloody glove was found in Simpson's yard competes with the hypothesis that Fuhrman planted the glove, just as the hypothesis that Furhman is credible competes that he lied because he wanted to frame Simpson. The evidence that Fuhrman was a racist provides a convincing explanation of why he would do so. In case study 1, explanatory

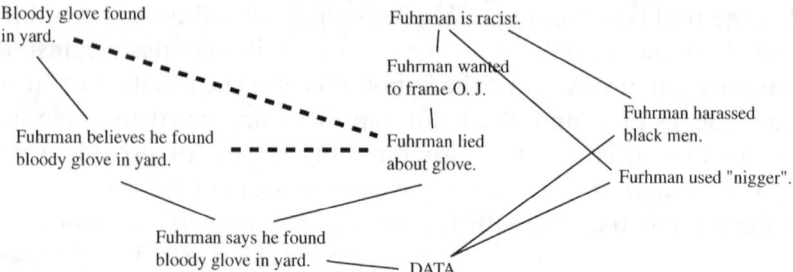

Figure 4. Explanatory-coherence analysis of why members of the jury in the trial of O. J. Simpson did not believe Fuhrman.

coherence explained why I believed Bioeye, and here it explains why members of the jury did not believe Fuhrman. Inferences about the credibility of Fuhrman are not shown in Figure 4, although they were surely made by the jury. Let us now investigate the nature of credibility in greater detail.

6. CREDIBILITY

As my discussion of Bioeye and Dandak indicated, the credibility of claimants is a crucial part of evaluating the claims that they make. But what is credibility and how is it assessed? This section argues first that the credibility of a speaker is not the same as reliability, which can be construed as a conditional probability. Rather, credibility should be understood as a dispositional psychological property of a person to be inferred by various means, including classification and analogy as well as enumerative induction.

The first crucial point to notice is that the credibility of a person is not a global property of the person, but is relative to particular topics (Fricker, 1995, p. 405). People may be credible on specific topics in which they have expertise, but not credible on other topics. For example, I have a friend who is a very reliable source of information on sports, but useless as a source on movies and politics. Bioeye was very credible on biological issues and questions involving developments at Oncolytics Biotech, but was caught out by other bulletin board members when she ventured opinions about legal matters involving patents. So whenever we speak of a person's credibility, we should consider it as relative to a particular topic. I shall use the formula $Cr(X,T)$ to represent the credibility of person X on topic T.

The simplest way of analyzing credibility would be as reliability construed as a conditional probability. Define $Rel(X, T)$ to be the probability that a claim on topic T is true given that it was made by person X, in symbols $P(C/X$ claims $C)$. Reliability can be understood as a frequency: the ratio of claims by X on topic T that turned out be true to all the claims made by X on topic T. For example, the reliability of Bioeye on biomedical information is the ratio of her true claims on this topic to all her claims. In principle, this kind of reliability could be calculated if one kept track of all her utterances on a topic and calculated what proportion of them are true. Presumably Bioeye would end up with a high reliability score while Dandak would have a low score. We might be tempted to posit the identity $Cr(X,T) = Rel(X,T)$.

There are several reasons why such an identification would be a mistake. First, we rarely have data that allow us to calculate reliability. An Internet bulletin board is unusual in that a reader could in principle look at all the claims made by a member over several years and then estimate what proportion are true. But even when such a record is available, no one has the time or interest to go back and make the calculation. In everyday life, there is no such permanent record of utterances so calculating a reliability ratio is impossible. Perhaps a person could do a rough estimate of a speaker's reliability based on a small sample of recent utterances, but people more commonly use such a sample to make explanatory inferences about a person's character, as described below.

The second reason for viewing credibility as different from reliability is that there are a number of different non-enumerative ways of inferring credibility. Consider, for example, Matdu1, a relatively new member of the board. When he (or she) began to post to the board in October 2001, I quickly recognized him as a credible source because of the kinds of biological information he presented. As the result of background research I did for my paper on Patrick Lee (Thagard, 2002), I knew enough about the biology that I could tell from content and style that Matdu1 knew what he was talking about. His posts resembled those of Bioeye in biological expertise. In contrast, here is a typical post from Dandak (May 7, 2002): "It is going DOWN, DOWN DOWN!!! I told you so! But you did not listen!!??@#%%$#@". BeammeupToddy was even worse (Jan. 14, 2002, *sic*): "ROFLMAO HOW STUPID can one pumper be??? You think someone will pay $8 a share for restricted stock in company with $3 share price, just suffer huge setback lose partner, and half only 21 months of cash left? GIVE YER HEAD A SHAKE BOY!!!" Both these quotes are exactly as they appeared in the Oncolytics Biotech bulletin board, and it should be obvious why no one would take them seriously. What little content they have is not backed by evidence, and the claims are poorly stated. In contrast, Bioeye and Matdul write well and convey information in defense of their claims. Hence, even though I have not calculated the reliability of Bioeye, Matdul, Dandak, and BeammeupToddy, I have no difficulty in judging the former two to be credible and the latter two not to be credible. Credibility is estimated on the basis of content and style as well as track record, not conditional probability. Presumably there is some correlation between credibility and reliability, but in evaluating testimony the former is prior to the latter. Content and style can speak directly to character and credibility, without intermediate probabilistic judgments of reliability. My judgments of reliability are not simply based on whether I like what the poster is saying, as there are people with positive posts that I ignore because they are poorly informed.

The third reason for not identifying credibility with reliability is that judgments concerning the two are affected very differently by the discovery that a person has uttered false statements. Suppose that a politician has made 100 statements about the economy, and it turns out that 2 of these are revealed to be false, where both of them concern an industry whose companies heavily contributed to the politician's campaign funds. The reliability of the politician on the economy would still be very high, 0.98, but we would become very reluctant to believe future utterances on this topic. It might even be said that the politician had, in the common phrase, "lost all credibility". Thus unlike reliability, credibility is not a simple linear function of the truth ratio of utterances. In the political case, we would infer that the politician has a set of beliefs and motivations that incline him or her to lie on topics relevant to the companies that provide financial support. Perhaps a mathematically sophisticated reasoner would think more extensively about whether the politician's 100 statements are statistically representative of all of his or her utterances, but the more natural inference is to judge the politician to be a liar with little credibility.

Thus credibility is not well construed as conditional probability, but rather requires a judgment about a person's disposition to tell the truth on a particular topic. Like all dispositions, we infer the existence of credibility by a theoretical inference to the best explanation. A person X is judged to be credible partly on the basis of X's track record on true statements, but also on the basis of the style and content of those utterances and our background knowledge about X. In general, X is judged to be credible if a disposition to tell the truth on a topic is inferred to be the best explanation of why X's utterances are usually true and have other desirable properties such as informativeness and comprehensibility. A judgment of credibility is thus itself based on explanatory coherence. In Bioeye's case, I have noticed a couple of instances where she reported misinformation, for example that the CEO of Oncolytics Biotech was still on the board of another company, Adherex. Rather than update Bioeye's reliability number, however, I made little alteration in my estimate of her credibility, since in this case she had clearly made a minor mistake based on not being aware of a recent change in the board of Adherex.

Figure 5 shows the structure of the judgment that Bioeye is credible, understood as a hypothesis about a dispositional property that can be ascribed to her. That Bioeye has this property is justified as the best explanation of the facts that she writes lucidly and informatively and is almost always correct in what she says. Figure 5 extends Figure 3 by having the node for credibility supported by evidence, rather than being treated as directly related to evidence. As in the earlier simulation of belief in Bioeye, the program ECHO concludes that she is right that the trial is done. The major difference between the two simulations is that here Bioeye's credibility is treated as an explanatory hypothesis rather than as given.

A similar account applies to the Mark Fuhrman case. Once the members of the Simpson jury learned that Furhman had lied about using the word "nigger" and had bragged about harassing black men, he lost all legal credibility. It was not just that his credibility received a numerical decrement as it would have if the juries had been making a judgment of reliability. Rather, the jury concluded that his character was fundamentally flawed so he was not to be believed in his testimony about Simpson.

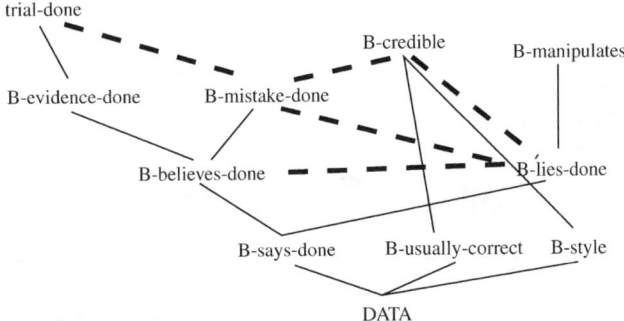

Figure 5. Full account of how a judgment about Bioeye's credibility influences the judgment that what she says is true.

Thus the importance of credibility does not support a probabilistic interpretation of testimony. Let us now look in more detail at the main probabilistic alternative to my explanatory-coherence theory of testimony.

7. THE BAYESIAN ALTERNATIVE

The theory of explanatory coherence and the computational model ECHO provide a thorough and exact version of the doctrine that causal reasoning is inference to the best explanation. The main alternative theory of causal reasoning is provided by Bayesian networks, which use the resources of probability theory along with recently developed algorithms for computing probabilities to model causal reasoning (Pearl, 1988, 2000). The Bayesian approach is elegant and powerful, but there are reasons to think that it does not have much application to human thinking (Thagard, 2000, ch. 8; 2004). I will not attempt here a general comparison of Bayesian vs. explanatory-coherence approaches, but will describe a Bayesian simulation of the reasoning displayed in Figure 3. A Bayesian approach to evaluating testimony has been pursued by Goldman (1999, ch. 4).

Computationally, my Bayesian simulation produces the same basic result that ECHO does, accepting the hypothesis that Bioeye is right that the trial is done. Figure 6 shows the structure of the Bayesian network used in my simulations; it was produced using the program JavaBayes, an easy-to-use program due to Cozman (2001).

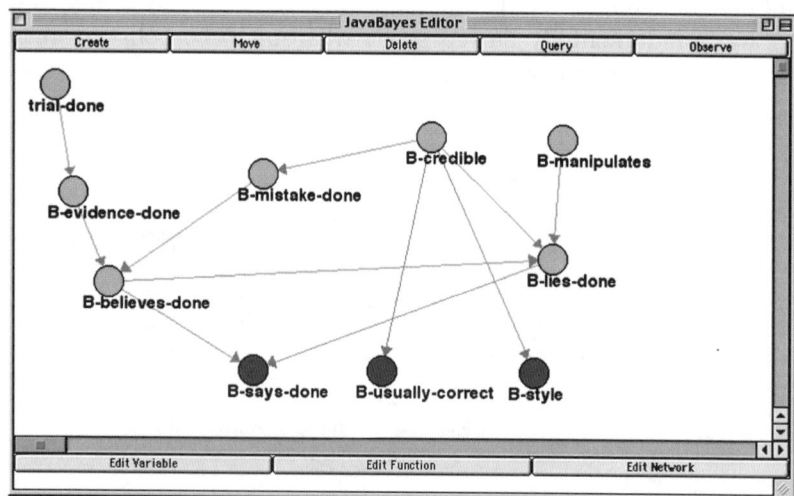

Figure 6. Bayesian simulation of the credibility of Bioeye using JavaBayes (Cozman, 2001). Arrows indicate causality.

To produce this simulation, I first had to identify the relevant nodes representing variables, which were adapted from the analysis in Appendix A. Next, I had to establish causal connections between nodes, which were also adapted from the explanation and contradiction relations in Appendix A. Finally, with much greater difficulty, I had to specify for each node with one or more arrows going into it the relevant conditional probabilities.

There are several reasons why the simulation in Figure 6 is implausible as an account of human thinking about the credibility of testimony. First, the simulation requires a host of conditional probabilities that people would be hard pressed to specify. Setting up the network requires specifying such conditional probabilities as P(B has evidence that the trial is done/trial is done), and also more complex ones. Because there are three arrows going into the node for *B-lies-done*, defining the function for calculating its probability requires specifying eight conditional probabilities, for example the probability that *B-lies-done* is false given that *B-manipulates* is true, *B-believes-done* is false, and *B-credible* is true. Despite having a reasonably good understanding of probabilities in domains where there are samples from populations of events, I have only the foggiest idea of what numbers to plug into the network. My rough guesses did, however, produce the desired result that the simulation concludes that the trial is done. Second, it is not clear what interpretation of probability to use. For epistemological purposes, it would be desirable to have objective probabilities, but these are only well defined for frequencies of occurrences in specified populations of events. Alternatively, a Bayesian might claim to be working with subjective probabilities understood as degrees of belief, but there is abundant psychological evidence that people's degrees of belief do not usually conform to the theory of probability (e.g. Kahneman et al., 1982; Gilovich et al., 2002). Third, it is not clear that the network in Figure 6 is a legitimate Bayesian network, because it is hard to say whether the links involve the direct causal influence that such networks require. Moreover, given the difficulty of assessing the relevant kinds of probabilities, it is impossible to determine whether the network satisfies the Markov condition that "a variable represented by a node in the Bayesian Network is independent of all variables represented by its non-descendant nodes in the Bayesian Network, conditional on all variables represented by its parent nodes" (Bovens and Hartman, 2003, p. 69). Hence it is not obvious that an explanatory coherence network can be translated into a Bayesian network so easily as Figure 6 suggests. For further discussion of the relevant applicability of

Bayesian and explanatory coherence approaches to legal reasoning, see Thagard (2004).

I see explanatory coherence as an alternative to Bayesian epistemology, in contrast to theorists who assess coherentist epistemology within the framework of Bayesian networks (Bovens and Olsson, 2000; Olsson,2002a, b; Bovens and Hartman, 2003). Given the difficulty of interpreting and assigning probabilities to statements in law, science, and everyday life, there is no reason to take Bayesian theory as canonical. In particular, both the descriptive and normative theories of testimony can more plausibly be based on explanatory coherence rather than probabilistic ideas. In contrast, Lipton (2001) argues for the compatibility of probabilistic and explanatory analyses.

8. THE JUSTIFICATION OF TESTIMONY-BASED BELIEF

To conclude, I address the general question of how belief based on testimony is justified. Following a distinction made by Coady (1992), approaches to justification can be classified as *reductionist* or *non-reductionist*. Reductionist views hold that the justification of beliefs based on testimony is not special to testimony, but rather relies on the independent justifiability of beliefs based on perception, memory, or inductive inference. Reductionists in this sense include Hume (1972), Fricker (1994, 1995), Lipton (1998), and Lyons (1997). Non-reductionists maintain that acceptance of testimony is justified in itself, unless there is some reason to think that the testimony is false. Reasons for holding a non-reductionist view range from the contention by Reid (1970) that God created people with a propensity to speak the truth to a kind of transcendental argument that if testimony were not reliable there would be no such thing as testimony (Coady, 1992).

My dual-pathway model of response to testimony-based belief is reductionist, in that both pathways depend prescriptively on kinds of inference that are broadly used in domains other than testimony. Consider first the default pathway. It may well be that the tendency for people to believe what they are told is innate, not because of divine providence, but because of natural selection. We can at least tell a story of human evolution that involves selection for people who generally tell the truth as well as for people who generally believe what they are told. Groups of such individuals would likely have been more successful in surviving and reproducing than groups consisting primarily of the duplicitous and incredulous. Human society does include psychopaths who are adept at and enthusiastic about lying, but such people are less than 1% of the population (Hare, 1993). If it seems plausible that the vast majority of statements made by people and media sources are true, then the default pathway is fairly reliable as well as efficient. Evolution, then, provided people with the default pathway that is useful both socially and epistemically. I do not know whether this story is true, but it does suggest how the default pathway to testimony-based inference might be both innate and reliable. The study by Feldman, Forrest, and Happ (2002) that found frequent lying may not be representative of most social interactions, because it involved participants who were strangers to each other and who were instructed to present themselves as likeable and competent.

What about the reflective pathway? If reflection about testimony depends on explanatory coherence, then its justification is the same as such inference in general. As I argued at the end of Section 7, I do not think that the justification of explanatory inferences depends on some Bayesian inference that they produce probable conclusions. Rather the justification of people's use of explanatory coherence is more indirect. Scientists' use of inference to the best explanation can be justified by noting that it is a standard practice in scientific thinking, and that there is much evidence from the technological applications of science that it often produce theories that succeed in representing how the world really is. A similar justification might be given for use in ordinary social contexts: we frequently use inference to the best explanation to infer the mental states of others, and the frequent successes of social interactions show that this strategy must be at least approximately veridical. Whatever justification applies to inference to the best explanation based on explanatory coherence applies by extension to testimony-based inference of the sort I described. Of course, such inferences are sometimes mistaken, like all inductive inferences, but the general practice of explanatory-coherence-based inference, in testimony and other contexts, is legitimated.

In sum, my dual-pathway account of testimony-based inference is consistent with a reductionist view of testimony that deems it to be justified on general inductive grounds. Neither Reid's divine inter- vention nor Coady's transcendental argument is needed to justify our very general practice of believing what we are told. My form of reductionist justification is complicated, however, by the fact that it gives different inductive justifications for each of the default and reflective pathways. When someone tells you something, whether you do and should believe it depends on what you know about the claim and the person making it.

ACKNOWLEDGMENTS

I am grateful to Luc Bovens, Axel Gelfert, Peter Lipton, Erik Olsson and anonymous referees for comments on earlier drafts. The research was supported by the Natural Sciences and Engineering Research Council of Canada.

APPENDIX A: INPUT TO ECHO SIMULATION OF INFERENCE
ABOUT BIOEYE

---

1. Input for simulation of network in Figure 2

(proposition 'trial-done "Clinical trial completed.")
(proposition 'B-says-done "Bioeye says trial completed.")
(proposition 'B-lies-done "Bioeye lies about trial.")
(proposition 'B-manipulates "Bioeye wants stock up.")
(proposition 'B-believes-done "Bioeye believes trial is done.")
(proposition 'B-mistake-done "Bioeye is mistaken.")
(proposition 'B-evidence-done "Bioeye has evidence trial is done.")
(proposition 'B-cred-sci "Bioeye is credible about science.")
; alternative explanations
(explain '(B-believes-done) 'B-says-done)
(explain '(B-lies-done) 'B-says-done)
(explain '(B-evidence-done) 'B-believes-done)
(explain '(B-mistake-done) 'B-believes-done)
(explain '(trial-done) 'B-evidence-done)
(explain '(B-manipulates) 'B-lies-done)
; contradictions
(contradict 'B-lies-done 'B-believes-done)
(contradict 'B-lies-done 'trial-done)
; the evidence
(data '(B-says-done))
2. Additional input for simulation in Figure 3
(contradict 'B-cred-sci 'B-lies-done)
(contradict 'B-cred-sci 'B-mistake-done)
(data '(B-says-done B-cred-sci))
3. Alternative additional input for simulation in Figure 5
(explain '(B-cred-sci) 'B-style)
(explain '(B-cred-sci) 'B-usually-correct)
(contradict 'B-cred-sci 'B-lies-done)
(contradict 'B-cred-sci 'B-mistake-done)
(data '(B-says-done B-usually-correct B-style))

REFERENCES

Audi, R.: 1997, 'The Place of Testimony in the Fabric of Knowledge and Justification', *American Philosophical Quarterly* **34**, 405–422.

Bovens, L. and S. Hartman: 2003, *Bayesian Epistemology*, Clarendon Press, Oxford.

Bovens, L. and E. J. Olsson: 2000, 'Coherentism, Reliability, and Bayesian Networks', *Mind* **109**, 685–720.

Burge, T.: 1993, 'Content Preservation', *Philosophical Review* **102**, 457–488.

Coady, C. A. J.: 1992, *Testimony: A Philosophical Study*, Clarendon Press, Oxford

Cozman, F. J.: 2001, 'JavaBayes: Bayesian Networks in Java', http://www-2. cs.cmu.edu/~javabayes/.

Diller, A.: 2000, 'Evaluating Information Found in Journal Articles,' in A. J. Nepomuceno , F. Quesada and F.J. Salguero (eds.), *Logic, Language, and Information: Proceedings of the First Workshop on Logic and Language*, Editorial Kronos, Sevilla, pp. 71–78.

Feldman, R. S., J. A. Forrest and B. R. Happ: 2002, 'Self-Presentation and Verbal Deception: Do Self-presenters Lie More?', *Basic and Applied Social Psychology* **24**, 13–171.

Fricker, E.: 1994, 'Against gullibility,' in B. K. Matilal and A. Chakrabarti (eds.), *Knowing from Words*, Kluwer, Dordrecht, pp. 125–161.

Fricker, E.: 1995, 'Telling and Trusting: Reductionism and Anti-Reductionism in the Epistemology of Testimony', *Mind* **104**, 393–411.

Gilovich, T., D. Griffin and D. Kahneman (eds.): 2002, *Heuristics and Biases: The Psychology of Intuitive Judgment*, Cambridge University Press, Cambridge.

Goldman, A.: 1999, *Knowledge in a Social World*, Oxford University Press, Oxford

Hare, R. D.: 1993, *Without Conscience: The Disturbing World of the Psychopaths among Us*, Pocket Books, New York.

Hume, D.: 1972, *Enquiries Concerning Human Understanding and Concerning the Principles of Morals* (2nd edn), Oxford University Press, Oxford

Kahneman, D., P. Slovic and A. Tversky: 1982, *Judgment Under Uncertainty: Heuristics and Biases*, Cambridge University Press, New York.

Kunda, Z.: 1990, 'The Case for Motivated Inference', *Psychological Bulletin* **108**, 480–498.

Lipton, P.: 1998, 'The Epistemology of Testimony', *Studies in History and Philosophy of Science* **29**, 1–31.

Lipton, P.: 2001, 'Is Explanation a Guide to Inference? A Reply to Wesley C. Simon,' in G. Hon and S. S. Rakover (eds.), *Explanation: Theoretical Approaches and Applications*, Kluwer, Dordrecht, pp. 93–120.

Lyons, J.: 1997, 'Testimony, Induction, and Folk Psychology', *Australasian Journal of Philosophy* **75**, 163–178.

Olsson, E. J.: 2002a, 'Corroborating Testimony, Probability, and Surprise', *British Journal for the Philosophy of Science* **53**, 273–288.

Olsson, E. J.: 2002b, 'What Is the Problem of Coherence and Truth?', *Journal of Philosophy* **99**, 246–272.

Pearl, J.: 1988, *Probabilistic Reasoning in Intelligent Systems*, Morgan Kaufman, San Mateo.

Pearl, J.: 2000, *Causality: Models, Reasoning, and Inference*, Cambridge University Press, Cambridge.

Reid, T.: 1970, *An Inquiry Into the Human Mind*, University of Chicago Press, Chicago.

Schiller, L. and J. Willwerth: 1997, *American Tragedy: The Uncensored Story of the Simpson Defense*, Avon Books, New York.

Thagard, P.: 1989, 'Explanatory Coherence', *Behavioral and Brain Sciences* **12**, 435–467.

Thagard, P.: 1999, *How Scientists Explain Disease*, Princeton University Press, Princeton.

Thagard, P.: 2000, *Coherence in Thought and Action*, MIT Press, Cambridge, MA

Thagard, P.: 2002, 'Curing Cancer? Patrick Lee's Path to the Reovirus Treatment', *International Studies in the Philosophy of Science* **16**, 179–193.

Thagard, P.: 2003, 'Why wasn't O.J. Convicted? Emotional Coherence in Legal Inference', *Cognition and Emotion* **17**, 361–383.

Thagard, P.: 2004, 'Causal Inference in Legal Decision Making: Explanatory Coherence vs. Bayesian networks', *Applied Artificial Intelligence* **18**, 231–249.

Department of Philosophy
University of Waterloo, Waterloo, Ont.,
Canada N2L 6G1
E-mail: pthagard@uwaterloo.ca

Erkenntnis (2005) 63:317–333
DOI 10.1007/s10670-005-4001-5

TOMOJI SHOGENJI

THE ROLE OF COHERENCE OF EVIDENCE IN THE NON-DYNAMIC MODEL OF CONFIRMATION

ABSTRACT. This paper examines the role of coherence of evidence in what I call the non-dynamic model of confirmation. It appears that other things being equal, a higher degree of coherence among pieces of evidence raises to a higher degree the probability of the proposition they support. I argue against this view on the basis of three related observations. First, we should be able to assess the impact of coherence on any hypothesis of interest the evidence supports. Second, the impact of coherence among the pieces of evidence can be different on different hypotheses of interest they support. Third, when we assess the impact of coherence on a hypothesis of interest, other conditions that should be held equal for a fair assessment include the degrees of individual support which the propositions directly supported by the respective pieces of evidence provide for the hypothesis. Once we take these points into consideration, the impression that coherence of evidence plays a positive role in confirmation dissipates. In some cases it can be shown that other things being equal, a higher degree of coherence among the pieces of evidence *reduces* the degree of confirmation for the hypothesis they support.

1. METHOD, MODEL AND THE THESIS

This paper examines the role of coherence of evidence in what I call the non-dynamic model of confirmation, where the tool of analysis is the probability calculus. Throughout this paper confirmation is understood in terms of prior and posterior probabilities of the hypothesis – namely, evidence E confirms hypothesis H if and only if $P(H|E) > P(H)$. The subject of this paper, the role of coherence of evidence, is to be distinguished from the role of coherence *between a hypothesis and the evidence*, which is often analyzed in terms of explanatory coherence, i.e., degrees to which the hypothesis explains the evidence. It is beyond reasonable doubt in my view that, other things being equal, the evidence confirms a hypothesis better if it is more coherent with the hypothesis. The subject of this paper, on the other hand, is the role of coherence *among* pieces of evidence. This does not mean that I set aside the evidence-hypothesis relation. One of my points in this paper is that the recent literature on the role of coherence among pieces of evidence (Bovens and Olsson, 2000; Olsson, 2002; Bovens and Hartman, 2003a, b) neglects an important part of the hypothesis-evidence relation.

It is necessary to make a brief remark first on the general approach that I take in this paper. There are two ways of conducting a probabilistic analysis of the role of coherence in confirmation. One of them starts with pre-theoretical intuitions we have about the concept of coherence, such as mutual support and symmetry. The analyst translates these pre-theoretical intuitions into the language of the probability calculus to formulate a probabilistic measure of coherence. The analyst will then investigate what roles the measure in question plays in the confirmation of a hypothesis. The other approach starts with pre-theoretical intuitions we have about the roles of coherence in confirmation. The analyst tries to come up with a probabilistic measure (or measures) of coherence suitable for these roles. In this second approach the measure chosen need not accommodate all our pre-theoretical intuitions about coherence as long as it can play the role (or the roles) we are interested in. In this paper I take the second approach, focusing on one particular role that coherence of evidence appears to play in the confirmation of a hypothesis. I believe this approach is more fruitful than the other one since people with different backgrounds – logicians, philosophers of science, epistemologists of the traditional kind – often have different "pre-theoretical" intuitions about coherence.[1]

We also need to determine the framework of discussion. We can distinguish two models of confirmation – the dynamic and non-dynamic models – in which the coherence of evidence may play a role. In the dynamic model (the Lewis–BonJour model)[2] our estimates of the degrees of reliability about the sources of evidence change as we accumulate more evidence in the process of confirmation. For example, a high degree of coherence among pieces of evidence obtained from independent sources may raise the probability that these sources are reliable. In the non-dynamic model, on the other hand, we take the degrees of reliability of the sources of evidence to be established already, and thus our estimates of the degrees of reliability remain the same throughout the process of confirmation. It still appears that a higher degree of coherence among pieces of evidence raises the probabilities more that the propositions supported by the evidence are true. In this paper, I restrict my attention to the role of coherence in the non-dynamic model of confirmation.[3] My goal in this paper is to show that coherence of evidence does not play the positive role it appears to play in the non-dynamic model of confirmation.

The following is a typical example in which coherence of evidence appears to have a positive impact on the confirmation of a hypothesis. Consider the two sets of reports on the identity of a certain computer hacker.

E_1: Informant #1 states [A_1] that the hacker grew up in Japan.
E_2: Informant #2 states [A_2] that the hacker lives in Japan.
E_3: Informant #3 states [A_3] that the hacker speaks Japanese.

E_1^*: Informant #1* states [A_1^*] that the hacker grew up in China.
E_2^*: Informant #2* states [A_2^*] that the hacker lives in India.
E_3^*: Informant #3* states [A_3^*] that the hacker speaks French.

Since the framework of discussion in this paper is the non-dynamic model of confirmation, I will assume that the degrees of reliability have already been established for all the informants, and that we need not revise them as we receive new reports. This applies to all subsequent examples. I will call propositions A_i and A_i^* that E_i and E_i^* directly support respectively, *content propositions*. What people commonly call coherence of evidence is coherence of the content propositions. For example, given the common background knowledge, there is clearly a sense in which the content propositions A_1, A_2 and A_3 are more coherent than the content propositions A_1^*, A_2^* and A_3^*. Note that this does not mean that E_1, E_2 and E_3 are more coherent (more supportive of each other) than E_1^*, E_2^* and E_3^*. That depends further on the reliability of the informants – e.g., E_1, E_2 and E_3 are no more coherent than E_1^*, E_2^* and E_3^* if the informants make their statements randomly. My primary concern in this paper is the impact of coherence of evidence *in the sense of coherence of the content propositions* on the confirmation of the hypothesis.

In the hacker example it appears that other things being equal, the content propositions A_1, A_2 and A_3 in the first case, which are more coherent, are more likely to be true than the content propositions A_1^*, A_2^* and A_3^* in the second case, which are less coherent. More generally, it appears that, other things being equal, a higher degree of coherence among the content propositions makes it more likely that they are true. The standard formulation of this idea is to take the conjunction of the content propositions to be the hypothesis and claim that evidence confirms this hypothesis better if the content propositions are more coherent (Bovens and Olsson, 2000; Olsson, 2002; Bovens and Hartmann, 2003a, b). For example, the hypotheses in the hacker case above are $H = A_1 \, \& \, A_2 \, \& \, A_3$ and $H^* = A_1^* \, \& \, A_2^* \, \& \, A_3^*$, and the evidence seems to confirm the hypothesis better, other things being equal, when the pieces of evidence are more coherent. In what follows I seek a probabilistic measure of coherence that formally validates this thesis – i.e., the thesis that pieces of evidence confirm the hypothesis they support better if they are more coherent. My claim is that the search for a suitable measure reveals that coherence of evidence does not play the role it appears to play.

2. PRELIMINARIES

There are some preliminary issues to settle. First, I assume that the sources of evidence are independent. The reason for this provision is obvious. If, for example, the second and the third informants in the first case of the hacker example obtained the first informant's report and produced their reports by inference from it (and if we know that), then we will not consider the high degree of coherence among the reports an indication of their likely truth. Reports that are dependent on other reports that are already taken into account do not strengthen the confirmation. We want to express the assumption of evidential independence in probabilistic terms, and there is a standard way to do so, namely:

> Evidence E_1 is independent of evidence E_2 with respect to proposition A if and only if A screens off E_1 from E_2 – i.e., $P(E_2|E_1$ & $A) = P(E_2|A)$ and $P(E_2|E_1$ & $\sim A) = P(E_2|\sim A)$.

The idea, intuitively, is that two independent pieces of evidence do not affect each other's probability *directly*. They affect each other's probability only through the proposition they both support. As a result, if the truth or falsity of the proposition they support is known, the two pieces of evidence do not affect each other's probability. With respect to the content propositions that different pieces of evidence support, I understand independence of evidence in the following way:

> Evidence $E_1, \ldots, E_n$ are independent of each other with respect to propositions $A_1, \ldots, A_n$ they support respectively if and only if for any $i = 1, \ldots, n$, A_i screens off E_i from any truth-functional compound of $E_1, \ldots, E_{i-1}, E_{i+1}, \ldots, E_n$.

I will assume in this paper that the sources of evidence are independent in this sense.

Next, we assume that each piece of evidence is *one-dimensional* evidence for the content proposition it directly supports in the sense that the evidence supports other propositions only through the content proposition.[4] For example, if the informants are reliable, evidence E_1 that the first informant states that the hacker grew up in Japan directly supports the content proposition A_1 that the hacker grew up in Japan. One-dimensionality of evidence does not prevent E_1 from supporting other propositions. E_1 may support proposition A_2 that the hacker speaks Japanese, but it does so only indirectly through A_1 – namely, because E_1 supports A_1 and A_1 in turn supports A_2.[5] This restriction has the consequence that if we are already certain that A_1 is true or false, E_1 has no impact on the probability of A_2. In other words, A_1 screens off E_1 from A_2. More generally, I understand one-dimensionality of evidence in the following way:

> Evidence $E_1, \ldots, E_n$ are one-dimensional evidence for propositions $A_1, \ldots, A_n$ they support respectively if and only if for any $i = 1, \ldots, n$, A_i screens off E_i from any truth-functional compound of $A_1, \ldots, A_{i-1}, A_{i+1}, \ldots, A_n$.

I will assume in this paper that all relevant pieces of evidence are one-dimensional in this sense.

There is one more preliminary issue to settle – namely, the extent of the 'other things being equal' qualification. What conditions should be held equal for a fair assessment of the impact of coherence on the posterior probability of the hypothesis? There are some conditions that should obviously be held equal. For example, the degrees of the reliability of the sources of evidence should be held equal for a fair comparison of the impact of coherence, for the degrees of reliability affect the posterior probability of the hypothesis independently of the degrees of coherence among the content propositions. For example, if informants #1, #2, and #3 in the first hacker case, who provide highly coherent reports, are known to be much less reliable than their counterparts #1[*], #2[*] and #3[*] in the second case, then the posterior probability of $H = A_1$ & A_2 & A_3 may be less than that of $H^* = A_1^*$ & A_2^* & A_3^* even if a higher degree of coherence has a positive impact on the posterior probability of the hypothesis. For this reason the degrees of reliability of the comparable sources of evidence should be held equal. We can express the general idea of when a condition needs to be held equal in the following principle:

(1) Condition C should be held equal for a fair assessment of the impact of coherence on the posterior probability of hypothesis H if C affects the posterior probability of H without affecting the degree of coherence.

Applications of this principle to particular conditions depend on how the degree of coherence is measured since a certain condition may affect the degree of coherence measured in one way, but not the degree of coherence measured in another way.

There are, on the other hand, some conditions that should not be held equal for obvious reasons. For example, we cannot hold any conditions equal if doing so would freeze up the degree of coherence. This is because if the degree of coherence is completely fixed as a result of holding a certain condition equal, then we cannot assess the impact of coherence on the posterior probability of the hypothesis by varying the degree of coherence among the content propositions. Thus, the following principle should be accepted:

(2) Condition C should be held equal for a fair assessment of the impact of coherence on the posterior probability of hypothesis H only if C affects the posterior probability of H but holding C equal allows the degree of coherence to vary.

Applications of this principle to particular conditions also depend on how the degree of coherence is measured since holding a certain condition equal may freeze up the degree of coherence measured in one way, but not the degree of coherence measured in another way.

The two principles (1) and (2) above determine the status of some conditions, but they leave the status of others open, for there are some conditions which *need not be* held equal by principle (1) but which *may be* held equal by principle (2). For example, the prior probability of the hypothesis (the conjunction of the content propositions) affects the posterior probability of the hypothesis, but it also affects the degrees of coherence according to most measures of coherence.[6] So, this condition *need not be* held equal by principle (1). However, holding it equal does not completely fix the degree of coherence. So, the condition *may be* held equal by principle (2). Should we hold this condition equal?

Olsson (2001, 2002) proposes a liberal approach to the effect that no condition should be held equal if it affects the degree of coherence. This amounts to recommending that:

(1*) Condition C should be held equal for a fair assessment of the impact of coherence on the posterior probability of hypothesis H *if and only if* C affects the posterior probability of H without affecting the degree of coherence.

In my view this principle is too liberal. In particular, it is quite appropriate in my view that we should hold the prior probability of the hypothesis equal even if it affects the degree of coherence. We can see the reason by the following analogy. Suppose we want to assess the impact of the amount of physical exercise on health. For a fair assessment it is reasonable to compare the posterior degrees of health among people who had (essentially) the same prior degree of health but did different amounts of physical exercise. However, the analogue of (1*) would not allow this comparison because the amount of exercise people can do is partly dependent on their prior degree of health. The prohibition seems unreasonable because we would then be unable to distinguish the effect of the amount of physical exercise on the posterior degree of health from the effect of the prior degree of health. We should hold the prior degree of health equal since people with the same prior degree of health can still do different amounts of physical exercise and these amounts can affect their posterior degrees of health. In the same way it is reasonable to hold the prior probability of the hypothesis equal even if the degree of coherence is partly dependent on the prior probability of the hypothesis since the degree of coherence can vary even if the prior probability of the hypothesis is held equal. This enables us to distinguish the effect of the degree of coherence on the posterior probability of the hypothesis from the effect of the prior probability of the hypothesis. More generally, in order to isolate the effect of the degree of coherence, I favor the conservative approach of holding all conditions that affect the posterior probability of the hypothesis equal unless doing so freezes up the degree of coherence. This amounts to recommending that:

(2*) Condition C should be held equal for a fair assessment of the impact of coherence on the posterior probability of hypothesis H *if and only if* C affects the posterior probability of H but holding C equal allows the degree of coherence to vary.

Again, applications of this principle to particular conditions depend on how the degree of coherence is measured, but it is safe to hold equal the number of the pieces of evidence and the prior probability of the hypothesis (the conjunction of the content propositions) because they do not completely fix the degree of coherence.

The following is then the apparent role of coherence in the non-dynamic model of confirmation:

Coherence Thesis (standard formulation): Given the independence and one-dimensionality of all relevant pieces of evidence, and given the same number of the pieces of evidence, the same degrees of the reliability of the sources of evidence, and the same prior probability of the hypothesis (the conjunction of the content propositions), a higher degree of coherence among the content propositions makes it more likely that the hypothesis is true.

My reasoning below takes the form of *reductio ad absurdum*. To validate the coherence thesis, the degree of coherence needs to be measured in a certain way and the impact of coherence needs to be assessed in a certain way, and this leads to the discovery that coherence of evidence does not play the role it appears to play.

3. COHERENCE AND INCONSISTENCY

In this section, I argue against the standard formulation of the coherence thesis that takes the conjunction of the content propositions to be the hypothesis to confirm. I will begin with a general description of my reasoning against the standard formulation, and proceed to present a concrete example to illustrate my point. I will also mention some consequences of abandoning the standard formulation of the coherence thesis.

My first point is that in order for coherence of evidence to play the positive role it appears to play, the sources of evidence must be less than perfectly reliable. This is because if they are perfectly reliable, all the content propositions are true with certainty, which leaves no room for coherence to raise the probability of their conjunction. My next point is that if the sources of evidence are less than perfectly reliable, then sooner or later some inconsistency will arise among pieces of evidence. In other words, inconsistency among pieces of evidence is not an anomaly but something we should expect in normal cases of confirmation when the sources of evidence are less than perfectly reliable. There is nothing controversial in these points, but they reveal a problem in the standard formulation of the coherence thesis. The standard formulation takes the conjunction of the content propositions to be the hypothesis to confirm, but this makes any case involving inconsistent evidence (inconsistent content propositions) irrelevant to confirmation, for no amount of evidence can confirm an inconsistent hypothesis. The problem is that those cases that are made irrelevant by the standard formulation of the coherence thesis are normal cases of confirmation since inconsistency is something we should expect when the sources of evidence are less than perfectly reliable. It is surely unreasonable to throw out a case because of a single piece of evidence that makes the conjunction of the content propositions inconsistent when all other pieces of evidence are mutually supportive and pointing to the truth of a certain proposition. We should be able to take that proposition to be the hypothesis instead of the inconsistent conjunction of the content propositions, and consider the evidence coherent overall even if it is inconsistent due to a single piece of evidence.

We can see this point in the following example. Consider the two sets of reports below on the toss of a fair coin, where we assume that all the informants are reliable to the degree .8.

E_1: Informant #1 states [A_1] that the coin landed on Heads.
E_2: Informant #2 states [A_2] that the coin landed on Heads.
E_3: Informant #3 states [A_3] that the coin landed on Heads.
E_4: Informant #4 states [A_4] that the coin landed on Heads.
E_5: Informant #5 states [A_5] that the coin landed on Tails.

E_1^*: Informant #1* states [A_1^*] that the coin landed on Heads.
E_2^*: Informant #2* states [A_2^*] that the coin landed on Heads.
E_3^*: Informant #3* states [A_3^*] that the coin landed on Heads.
E_4^*: Informant #4* states [A_4^*] that the coin landed on Tails.
E_5^*: Informant #5* states [A_5^*] that the coin landed on Tails.

Since all the informants are reliable to the degree .8, the first set of reports, in which 80% of informants are in agreement, is a normal case we would most naturally expect. Further, despite their inconsistency, the content propositions in the first case do seem to "hang together" better than those in the second case. There is, in other words, a sense in which the content propositions in the first case are more coherent than those in the second case, and the overall evidence in the first case clearly points to the truth of the proposition H that the coin landed on Heads. Indeed, given the independence of the evidence, we obtain by Bayes's theorem $P(H|E_1 \& \ldots \& E_5) = .9846154$ for the first case and $P(H |E_1^* \& \ldots \& E_5^*) = .8$ for the second case.[7]

The standard formulation of the coherence thesis throws out numerous normal cases of confirmation, including the coin toss cases above where coherence of evidence appears to be as relevant to confirmation as it is in the hacker example. The standard formulation of the coherence thesis is therefore unreasonably restrictive. I propose to abandon the requirement that the hypothesis to confirm must be the conjunction of the content propositions. My position is not that we should never assess the impact of coherence on the conjunction of the content propositions. We can do so meaningfully when they are consistent. The point is that the conjunction of the content propositions is one of many propositions we can choose as our hypothesis. If we like, we can also assess the impact of coherence of evidence on the *disjunction* of the content propositions. In fact we can assess the impact of coherence of evidence on any hypothesis of our interest.

I have proposed to abandon the standard formulation of the coherence thesis so that the coherence thesis applies to cases involving inconsistent evidence. This proposal has two significant consequences. First, we cannot regard all inconsistent sets of content propositions as maximally incoherent. We need to differentiate inconsistent sets of content propositions by their different degrees of coherence. Many people have the pre-theoretical intuition that inconsistency is the extreme case of incoherence. If that is the case, no set of propositions is more incoherent than an inconsistent set of propositions. If we respect this intuition, an inconsistent set of propositions should receive the lowest possible degree of coherence. However, in order to apply the coherence thesis in many normal cases involving inconsistent evidence, we need to ignore this pre-theoretical intuition and assign different degrees of coherence to different inconsistent sets of propositions. There are many ways of doing so. One way is to make use of pair-wise coherence. In the coin toss example, more content propositions in the first case are pair-wise coherent than those in the second case. I should note that those interested in explanatory coherence often take this pair-wise approach (most notably Thagard, 1992, 2000). I once criticized the pair-wise approach for the reason that an inconsistent set can be pair-wise coherent and receive a positive degree of coherence in the pair-wise approach (Shogenji, 1999). This seems counterintuitive, but if coherence is to play the role it appears to play in normal cases of confirmation, we cannot preserve all our pre-theoretical intuitions about coherence.

Another significant consequence of abandoning the standard formulation of the coherence thesis is that the impact of coherence is different on different hypotheses of interest. We can no longer say simply that coherence among the content propositions makes *the* hypothesis more likely to be true. Coherence of evidence may have a positive impact on the posterior probability of one hypothesis, but have a negative impact on that of a different hypothesis. This is so even if we restrict our attention to the content propositions. For example, if most of the content propositions hang together tightly while a few are incoherent with them, we expect the impact of their overall coherence to be different on members of these two groups of content propositions. The first case in the coin toss example illustrates this point. The evidence sharply raises the probability of proposition H that the coin landed on Heads, but sharply lowers the probability of proposition T that the coin landed on Tails. Our next task is to account for this difference.

The difference in the posterior probabilities of H and T cannot be due to any difference in the degree of coherence among the content propositions, for we are focusing on a single set of reports, E_1, E_2, E_3, E_4 and E_5, and their respective content propositions, A_1, A_2, A_3, A_4 and A_5. The same set of reports cannot have different degrees of coherence among themselves for H and for T. For the same reason, the difference between posterior probabilities of H and T cannot be due to any difference in the number of reports, or any difference in the degrees of reliability of the informants. We also assumed that H and T have the same prior probabilities. This means that there is a condition that has been neglected so far that affects the posterior probability of the hypothesis – namely, the degrees of support the content propositions provide *individually* for the hypothesis of interest. In the first case of the coin toss example, four of the five content propositions individually support H, while only one content proposition individually supports T. It is because of this difference that the evidence sharply raises the probability of H but sharply lowers the probability of T. All other conditions are the same, including the degree of coherence among the content propositions.

This leads to the following observation: for a fair assessment of the impact of coherence *per se* on the posterior probability of the hypothesis, the conditions that should be held equal include the degrees of support the content propositions provide individually for the hypotheses of interest, H and H^*, that we are comparing – i.e., $P(H|A_i) = P(H^*|A_i^*)$ for all $i = 1, \ldots, n$.[8] I also want to note that this point of holding equal the degrees of individual support for the hypothesis applies even when we choose as our hypothesis the conjunction of the content propositions as required in the standard formulation of the coherence thesis. This point has been overlooked by those who adopt the standard formulation of the coherence thesis (Bovens and Olsson, 2000; Olsson, 2002; Bovens and Hartman, 2003a, b) because the standard formulation forces us to focus exclusively on the conjunction of the content propositions without considering other hypotheses, which may receive different degrees of individual support from the content propositions. They hold the degrees of reliability equal – i.e., $P(A_i|E_i) = P(A_i^*|E_i^*)$ – but support that individual pieces of evidence provide for their respective content propositions is only one part of support they provide for the hypothesis. The other part is support the individual content propositions in turn provide for the hypothesis. The standard formulation of the coherence thesis is silent on this second part, $P(H|A_i)$ and $P(H^*|A_i^*)$, which are respectively $P(A_1 \& \ldots \& A_n|A_i)$ and $P(A_1^* \& \ldots \& A_n^*| A_i^*)$. When the restriction of the standard formulation on the choice of the hypothesis is removed, it becomes obvious that we should take into account the degrees of support the content propositions provide individually for the hypothesis as a factor that is distinct from the degree of coherence among the content propositions, and we cannot ignore this factor even if we choose the conjunction of the content propositions as our hypothesis.

4. THE DEMISE OF THE COHERENCE THESIS

I have made three related observations about the apparent role of coherence of evidence in the non-dynamic model of confirmation. First, the standard formulation of the coherence thesis that takes the hypothesis to be the conjunction of the content propositions is too restrictive. We should be able to assess the impact of coherence on the posterior probability of any hypothesis of interest. Second, the impact of coherence on the posterior probability can be different for different hypotheses we choose. Third, for a fair assessment of the impact of coherence on the posterior probability of the hypothesis, other conditions that should be held equal include the degrees of support the content propositions provide individually for the hypothesis. In this final section, I will show that once we take these points into consideration, the impression that coherence of evidence plays a positive role in the non-dynamic model of confirmation dissipates. I will also provide an example in which other things being equal, a higher degree of coherence (by any reasonable measure) among the pieces of evidence *reduces* the degree of the confirmation of the hypothesis.

Let us see first how the impression of the positive role of coherence dissipates. Recall the hacker example from Section 1, where a higher degree of coherence appears to raise more the probability of the conjunction of the content propositions. Let us take the conjunctions $A_1 \& A_2 \& A_3$ and $A_1^* \& A_2^* \& A_3^*$ to be hypotheses H and H^*, respectively, as suggested by the standard formulation. I grant that the content propositions A_1, A_2 and A_3 in the first case are more coherent than A_1^*, A_2^* and A_3^* in the second case. I also grant that the posterior probability of hypothesis H is higher than the posterior probability of hypothesis H^*, i.e., $P(H|E_1 \& E_2 \& E_3) > P(H^*|E_1^* \& E_2^* \& E_3^*)$.

However, it is premature to conclude that coherence of evidence plays a positive role in the confirmation of the hypothesis. The problem is that one crucial condition that should be held equal for a fair comparison is not the same in the example. Namely, content propositions A_1, A_2 and A_3 in the first case provide more *individual support* for H than A_1^*, A_2^* and A_3^* do for H^* in the second case – i.e., $P(H|A_1) > P(H^*|A_1^*)$, $P(H|A_2) > P(H^*|A_2^*)$ and $P(H|A_3) > P(H^*|A_3^*)$. For example, A_1 alone (that the hacker grew up in Japan) already supports H (that the hacker grew up in Japan, lives in Japan, and speaks Japanese) quite strongly, while A_1^* alone (that the hacker grew up in China) hardly supports H^* (that the hacker grew up in China, lives in India, and speaks French). It is thus unclear what the impact of coherence *per se* is in this example. The higher posterior probability of the hypothesis in the first case may be entirely a result of the higher degrees of support that the content propositions provide individually for the hypothesis.

For a fair assessment of the impact of coherence *per se*, we need to compare the posterior probabilities of the hypotheses in comparable cases where the degrees of coherence are different but the hypotheses receive the same degrees of support from the individual content propositions. Such comparison is not easy to obtain since other things being equal, the degrees of individual support tend to be greater when the content propositions are more coherent. However, a higher degree of coherence and greater degrees of support that the content propositions provide individually for the hypothesis do not always come together. I now describe a pair of cases where the degrees of coherence are different but the degrees of support that the content propositions provide individually for the hypothesis (as well as other conditions to be held equal for a fair comparison) are the same.

The contestant on a quiz show has to choose the correct answer from four choices 1, 2, 3 and 4. She has no clue as to which is the correct answer, so prior probabilities are the same for the four answers. The contestant has two informants available, each of whom has the degree of reliability .8. Compare the following two cases.

E_1: Informant #1 states [A_1] that an even-numbered answer is correct.
E_2: Informant #2 states [A_2] that an even-numbered answer is correct.

E_1^*: Informant #1* states [A_1^*] that an even-numbered answer is correct.
E_2^*: Informant #2* states [A_2^*] that a prime-numbered answer is correct.

By any reasonable measure of coherence the content propositions A_1 and A_2, which are in complete agreement, have a greater degree of coherence than A_1^* and A_2^*, which are probabilistically independent. Prior probabilities of the content propositions are all .5. Further, if we choose as our hypothesis, $H = H^*$, the proposition that the correct answer is 2,[9] then the degrees of individual support that the hypothesis receives from A_1, A_2, A_1^* and A_2^* are the same – i.e., $P(H|A_1) = P(H|A_2) = P(H^*|A_1^*) = P(H^*|A_2^*) = .5$.

The example is constructed so that all relevant conditions are the same between the two cases except for the degrees of coherence. We should therefore be able to assess the impact of coherence *per se* on the probability of the hypothesis by comparing the posterior probabilities, $P(H|E_1 \ \& \ E_2)$ and $P(H^*|E_1^* \ \& \ E_2^*)$. The calculation is straightforward. From the independence of evidence and $A_1 = A_2$, we obtain $P(E_1 \ \& \ E_2|A_1) = P(E_1|A_1) \times P(E_2|A_2) = r^2$ and $P(E_1 \ \& \ E_2|\sim A_1) = P(E_1|\sim A_1) \times P(E_2|\sim A_2) = (1 - r)^2$, where r is the reliability of the informants, which we assume to be .8. By Bayes's Theorem $P(A_1|E_1 \ \& \ E_2) = r^2/(r^2 + (1 - r)^2) = .64/.68$, hence $P(H|E_1 \ \& \ E_2) = 1/2 \times .64/.68 \approx .47$. Meanwhile since E_1^* and E_2^* are one-dimensional evidence for A_1^* and A_2^*, respectively, and since A_1^* and A_2^* are probabilistically independent, $P(A_1^*|E_1^* \ \& \ E_2^*) = P(A_1|E_1^*) = r$ and $P(A_2^*|E_1^* \ \& \ E_2^*) = P(A_2^*|E_2^*) = r$. Further, since $H^* = A_1^* \ \& \ A_2^*$, and since A_1^* and A_2^* are probabilistically independent, $P(H^*|E_1^* \ \& \ E_2^*) = P(A_1^*|E_1^* \ \& \ E_2^*) \times P(A_2^*|E_1^* \ \& \ E_2^*) = r^2 = .64$. This means that all other things being equal, the hypothesis is confirmed *better* when the content propositions are *less* coherent. There is a way of grasping this result without carrying out the calculation. If all informants are extremely reliable, then both $P(A_1 \ \& \ A_2|E_1 \ \& \ E_2)$ and $P(A_1^* \ \& \ A_2^*|E_1^* \ \& \ E_2^*)$ are near certainty, but H is much stronger than $A_1 \ \& \ A_2$ in that it admits only half of the possibilities that the latter admits, while H^* is simply $A_1^* \ \& \ A_2^*$. So, the posterior probability of H in the first case is lower than a half while the posterior probability of H^* in the second case is near certainty. As a result, H^* in the second case, in which the content propositions are less coherent, is confirmed better than H in the first case, in which the content propositions are more coherent.

One way of informally explaining this result is that highly coherent (strongly mutually supportive) propositions tend to have similar contents,[10] and thus their conjunction does not carry much more information than each of its conjuncts does. The first case in the quiz show example is an extreme case where the conjunction is identical to each of its conjuncts. As a result, when a single piece of evidence already supports one of the conjuncts strongly and hence supporting the conjunction strongly as well, the second piece of evidence supporting the other conjunct is largely redundant for the purpose of confirmation. In contrast the conjunction of less coherent propositions tends to carry much more information than each of its conjuncts does, as in the second case of the quiz show example. Consequently, even if the first piece of evidence supports one of the conjuncts strongly, the second piece of evidence is hardly redundant. In short, when pieces of evidence support their respective content propositions strongly and the content propositions are highly coherent, there is a tendency that a significant part of the evidence is wasted because of the high level of redundancy, whereas all pieces of evidence tend to be utilized more fully when the content propositions are less coherent. It is therefore no surprise that in some cases in which all other conditions are equal, the hypothesis is confirmed *better* by the pieces of evidence that are *less* coherent.

To conclude, the coherence thesis is false. It looks correct because of the difficulty of distinguishing coherence of evidence on one hand and individual support that the content propositions provide for the hypothesis on the other, especially when we choose as our hypothesis the conjunction of the content propositions as in the standard formulation of the coherence thesis.

ACKNOWLEDGEMENTS

A precursor of this paper was presented at Workshop "Coherence" held in Bielefeld, Germany in September 2003. I would like to thank the organizer Ulrich Gähde and the participants of the workshop for the stimulating discussion. I am particularly grateful to one participant, who later served as an anonymous referee for this volume, for valuable written comments. I also benefited greatly from detailed and insightful comments by an anonymous referee for *Erkenntnis*.

NOTES

[1] I learned this from some objections (Akiba, 2000; Fitelson, 2003) raised against the probabilistic measure of coherence I proposed in Shogenji (1999).
[2] See Lewis (1946, p. 346) and BonJour (1985, p. 148).
[3] See Shogenji (2005) for a probabilistic analysis of the role of coherence in the dynamic model of confirmation.

[4] Some authors (e.g., Bovens and Olsson, 2000; Bovens and Hartmann, 2003a, b) call the combination of what I call the 'independence' and 'one-dimensionality' of evidence simply the 'independence' of evidence. This is only a matter of different terminology.

[5] See Shogenji (2003) on the transitivity of probabilistic support under the condition that the evidence is one-dimensional.

[6] For example, by Shogenji's (1999) measure C_s, and by Olsson's (2002, p. 250) measure C_o:

$$C_s(A_1, \ldots, A_n) = \frac{P(A_1 \& \ldots \& A_n)}{P(A_1) \times \cdots \times P(A_n)}$$

$$C_o(A_1, \ldots, A_n) = \frac{P(A_1 \& \ldots \& A_n)}{P(A_1 \vee \cdots \vee A_n)}$$

[7] The former is from $P(E_1 \& \ldots \& E_5 | H) = P(E_1 | H) \times \cdots \times P(E_5 | H) = .8^4 \times .2$; $P(E_1 \& \ldots \& E_5 | \sim H) = P(E_1 | \sim H) \times \cdots P(E_5 | \sim H) = .2^4 \times .8$; and $P(H) = P(\sim H) = .5$. The latter is from $P(E_1^* \& \ldots \& E_5^* | H) = P(E_1^* | H) \times \cdots \times P(E_5^* | H) = .8^3 \times .2^2$; $P(E_1^* \& \ldots \& E_5^* | \sim H) = P(E_1^* | \sim H) \times \cdots \times P(E_5^* | \sim H) = .2^2 \times .8^3$; and $P(H) = P(\sim H) = .5$.

[8] I will present an example toward the end of Section 4 to show that when the degrees of support the content propositions provide individually for the hypothesis of interest are held equal, the degree of coherence can still vary. So, by principle (2^*) of the 'other things being equal' qualification, we should hold the degrees of support the content propositions provide individually for the hypothesis equal for a fair assessment of the impact of coherence on the posterior probability of the hypothesis.

[9] H is not the conjunction of E_1 and E_2, so the example does not respect the standard formulation of the coherence thesis.

[10] According to one measure of similarity (Myrvold 1996), the degree of similarity is the degree of coherence by Shogenji's (1999) measure of coherence.

REFERENCES

Akiba, K.: 2000, 'Shogenji's Probabilistic Measure of Coherence Is Incoherent', *Analysis* **60**, 356–359.

BonJour, L.: 1985, *The Structure of Empirical Knowledge*, Harvard University Press, Cambridge, MA.

Bovens, L. and S. Hartmann: 2003a, 'Solving the Riddle of Coherence', *Mind* **112**, 601–633.

Bovens, L. and S. Hartmann: 2003b, *Bayesian Epistemology*, Oxford University Press, Oxford.

Bovens, L. and E. J. Olsson: 2000, 'Coherence, Reliability and Bayesian Networks', *Mind* **109**, 685–719.

Fitelson, B.: 2003, 'A Probabilistic Theory of Coherence', *Analysis* **63**, 194–199.

Lewis, C. I.: 1946, *An Analysis of Knowledge and Valuation*, Open Court, LaSalle, IL.

Myrvold, W.: 1996, 'Bayesianism and Diverse Evidence: A Reply to Andrew Wayne', *Philosophy of Science* **63**, 661–665.

Olsson, E. J.: 2001, 'Why Coherence Is Not Truth Conducive', *Analysis* **61**, 236–241.

Olsson, E. J.: 2002, 'What is the Problem of Coherence and Truth?', *The Journal of Philosophy* **99**, 246–272.

Shogenji, T.: 1999, 'Is Coherence Truth Conducive?', *Analysis* **59**, 338–345.

Shogenji, T.: 2003, 'A Condition for Transitivity in Probabilistic Support', *The British Journal for the Philosophy of Science* **54**, 613–616.

Shogenji, T.: 2005, 'Justification by Coherence from Scratch', *Philosophical Studies* **125**, 305–325.

Thagard, P.: 1992, *Conceptual Revolutions*, Princeton University Press, Princeton.

Thagard, P.: 2000, *Coherence in Thought and Action*, MIT Press, Cambridge, MA.

Philosophy Department
Rhode Island College, Providence
RI 02908
USA
E-mail: tshogenji@ric.edu

Erkenntnis (2005) 63:335–360
DOI 10.1007/s10670-005-4002-4

MARK SIEBEL

AGAINST PROBABILISTIC MEASURES OF COHERENCE

ABSTRACT. It is shown that the probabilistic theories of coherence proposed up to now produce a number of counter-intuitive results. The last section provides some reasons for believing that *no* probabilistic measure will ever be able to adequately capture coherence. First, there can be no function whose arguments are nothing but tuples of probabilities, and which assigns different values to pairs of propositions {A, B} and {A, C} if A implies both B and C, or their negations, and if $P(B) = P(C)$. But such sets may indeed differ in their degree of coherence. Second, coherence is sensitive to explanatory relations between the propositions in question. Explanation, however, can hardly be captured solely in terms of probability.

Why does the proposition 'Tweety is a bird' fit 'Tweety has wings' much better than 'Tweety cannot fly'? Because, one might argue, the probability that Tweety has wings, given that it is a bird, strongly exceeds the probability that Tweety cannot fly, given that it is a bird. Presumably, such considerations have led some philosophers to develop *probabilistic* measures of coherence. Tomoji Shogenji, Erik Olsson, Branden Fitelson, and Igor Douven and Wouter Meijs have presented functions which take as input certain probabilities relating to the propositions in question to calculate from them a number which is supposed to represent their degree of coherence.[1]

In Sections 1–5, I point out some difficulties with these proposals as well as with Luc Bovens and Stephan Hartmann's coherence quasi-ordering. However, even if these specific accounts prove to be deficient, this does certainly not mean that the notion of a probabilistic measure of coherence is *fundamentally* wrong. After all, this research project is still in its infancy, and it thus seems justifiable to adopt a 'don't worry it'll sort itself out' attitude. In opposition to this attitude, the last section provides some grounds for believing that *no* probabilistic function will ever be able to adequately capture coherence.

1. SHOGENJI'S MEASURE

According to Shogenji (1999, p. 240), the coherence of a system of propositions $\{A_1, \ldots, A_n\}$ is to be determined as follows:

$$C_S(A_1, \ldots, A_n) = \frac{P(A_1 \ldots A_n)}{P(A_1) \times \cdots \times P(A_n)}$$

$P(A_1) \times \cdots \times P(A_n)$ is the probability the conjunction $A_1 \& \ldots \& A_n$ would have if its constituents were statistically independent. Shogenji's formula thus tells us to which extent the actual probability that the propositions are true together deviates from the probability they would have if they were statistically independent. If the C_S-value is greater than 1, the set is coherent; if it is smaller than 1, the statements do not fit together, where 0 means that they are maximally incoherent.

Note that all probabilistic measures have to confront the question of whether it is possible to determine the relevant probabilities in a satisfactory way when we are faced with concrete problems. For example, in order to apply Shogenji's proposal, we need the prior probabilities $P(A_1)$ to $P(A_n)$. But if one of the propositions at issue is a newly developed scientific theory, how to fix its probability? We might often be able to confer on it a probability in the Bayesian sense of a subjective degree of confidence; but many epistemologists are not satisfied with such an approach because it smacks of an 'it's all at your discretion' stance. However, I will not follow this train of thought and would rather make concessions to supporters of probabilistic epistemology by taking into account only cases where the relevant probabilities, or ratios thereof, are unproblematic. If a probabilistic measure of coherence fails here already because it leads to inadequate results, the question of its applicability to other cases may be considered to be of secondary importance.

Shogenji's measure is counter-intuitive for a number of reasons. First, let there be ten equiprobable suspects for a murder. All of them previously committed at least one crime, two a robbery, two pickpocketing, and the remaining six both crimes. There is thus a substantial overlap: of the total of eight suspects who committed a robbery, six were also involved in pickpocketing, and conversely. On account of this strong coincidence, I see no reason why the pair of propositions

(M1) The murderer committed a robbery.
(M2) The murderer committed pickpocketing.

should be regarded incoherent. But in the light of Shogenji's proposal:

$$C_S(M1, M2) = \frac{P(M1\ M2)}{P(M1) \times P(M2)} = \frac{0.6}{0.8 \times 0.8} < 1,$$

which would mean that these assumptions do not fit together.

Generally, when we are confronted with two statements which cannot both be false, Shogenji's function assigns them a coherence value of 1 at most. For if $\neg A$ implies B, then $\neg A$ is logically equivalent to $\neg A$ & B so that:

$$P(A) = 1 - P(\neg A) = 1 - P(\neg A\ B)$$
$$\geq 1 - \frac{P(\neg A\ B)}{P(B)} = 1 - P(\neg A|B) = P(A|B) = \frac{P(A\ B)}{P(B)}$$

Hence:

$$P(A\ B) \leq P(A) \times P(B)$$

But the fact that one of the assumptions in question must be true does not rule out that they cohere. In a nutshell, Shogenji's measure does not adequately treat subcontraries (cf. Siebel, 2004).

Second, Ken Akiba (2000, p. 357) has claimed that it is also on the wrong track with respect to two-member cases in which one of the propositions implies the other. If B logically follows from A, $P(A$ & $B)$ is identical with $P(A)$, entailing that $C_S(A, B) = 1/P(B)$. Thus, statements of this type would be the more coherent the less likely consequence B is. But the following example seems to suggest that this is a mistake (the die is, of course, meant to be fair):

(D1)   The die will come up 2.
(D2)   The die will come up 2 or 4.
(D3)   The die will come up 2, 4 or 6.

D2, so Akiba says, dovetails with D1 just as much as D3 does because both propositions are logical consequences of D1. According to Shogenji's function, however, the coherence of {D1, D2} is 3, whereas {D1, D3} is merely coherent to degree 2.

In order to show that such systems do differ in coherence, Shogenji (2001, p. 148) refers us to a similar example. A fossil is dated by three measurements. The results are:

(F1)   The fossil is 64–66 million years old.
(F2)   The fossil is 63–67 million years old.
(F3)   The fossil is more than 10 years old.

F1 implies both F2 and F3, and {F1, F2} is more coherent according to Shogenji's formula than {F1, F3} because $P(\text{F2}) < P(\text{F3})$. But this appears to be all right because, intuitively, F1 and F2 fit together better than F1 and F3. After all, '64--66 million years' is, in a natural sense, closer to '63--67 million years' than to 'more than 10 years' because the latter leaves open many more alternatives which are excluded by '64--66 million years'. For example, F3, but neither F1 nor F2, would be true if the fossil was 20 million years old. The same may be said to hold in the die example. The assumption that the die will come up 2 or 4 permits only one alternative not covered by D1, namely 4. On the other hand, the weaker assumption that the die will come up 2, 4 or 6 includes two possibilities running counter to D1. It thus appears reasonable to maintain that {D1, D2} registers a greater coherence than {D1, D3}.

So far, so good. But what about examples where the logical consequences comprise only *one* alternative to the proposition they follow from? Suppose a physicist cannot recall the voltage of a power source. She only knows that it is 1 V or 2 V or ... 50 V. She asks her assistants, and their answers are:

(V1)   The voltage is 1 V.
(V2)   The voltage is 1 or 2 V.
(V3)   The voltage is 1 or 50 V.

Since a voltage of 2 V is as likely as a voltage of 50 V, V2's probability does not differ from V3's. Shogenji is thus committed to the claim that V1 dovetails with V3 just as much as with V2: $C_S(\text{V1}, \text{V3}) = 1/P(\text{V3}) = 1/P(\text{V2}) = C_S(\text{V1}, \text{V2})$.

But this is not the way in which our physicist will appraise the coherence of these pairs. It would rather appear that V1 fits V2 more than V3 because V2's alternative is much closer to V1 than V3's alternative. If V1 is false because the voltage is 2 V, there is at least a close proximity to V1. But if it is false because the voltage is 50 V, then the truth is miles away from V1. Shogenji's purely probabilistic approach overlooks that coherence is also sensitive to such distances between numerical values, thereby ignoring an aspect which is highly important for scientists.

Third, assume again that the probability for 2 V is the same as for 50 V. This time, however, the statements put forward by the physicist's assistants cannot be true together:

(V4)   The voltage is 1 V.

(V5)   The voltage is 2 V.
(V6)   The voltage is 50 V.

On account of the inherent inconsistency, I am ready to grant that both {V4, V5} and {V4, V6} are *incoherent*. Nevertheless, the former set is *less* incoherent than the latter because 1 V is closer to 2 V than to 50 V. Presumably, our physicist will therefore disregard the possibility that the voltage is 50 V and assume that it is close to what the first two assistants have said. By applying Shogenji's measure, however, {V4, V5} and {V4, V6} would turn out to be incoherent to the same degree. Since V4 implies ¬V5 as well as ¬V6, P(V4 & V5) = P(V4 & V6) = 0. Hence, C_S(V4, V5) and C_S(V4, V6) are also 0, which means that these sets are indistinguishable with respect to coherence because they are both maximally incoherent.

More generally, I do not deny that inconsistencies have a negative *influence* on coherence. It might even be the case that propositions are coherent only if they are consistent (cf. BonJour 1985, p. 95). But this does not entail that contrary propositions make a system incoherent *to the maximum*. There may be further factors present which have a positive impact and thus partly compensate for inconsistencies. A closer proximity of numerical values is one such factor. By rendering sets of contrary statements maximally incoherent, Shogenji does not take into account this aspect of coherence, although it plays a significant role in scientific thinking.

Finally, Shogenji's measure entails that, by including the conjunction or disjunction of the propositions in question, coherence is usually increased. In the normal course of events, $P(A \& B)$ and $P(A \lor B)$ are smaller than 1. Moreover, both $A \& B \& (A \& B)$ and $A \& B \& (A \lor B)$ can be reduced to $A \& B$. Therefore:

$$C_S(A, B, A\ B) = \frac{P(A\ B)}{P(A) \times P(B) \times P(A\ B)} = \frac{C_S(A\ B)}{P(A\ B)}$$
$$> C_S(A, B)$$

$$C_S(A, B, A \lor B) = \frac{P(A\ B)}{P(A) \times P(B) \times P(A \lor B)} = \frac{C_S(A\ B)}{P(A \lor B)}$$
$$> C_S(A, B)$$

But this is not acceptable as a general rule. There might be scenarios in which the extended set can be taken to be more coherent. For example, let there be two witnesses, one of them asserting that the murderer is blonde and the second reporting that he spoke with a Scandinavian accent. These propositions fit together quite well; but if

[47]

a third witness appears claiming that the culprit is a blonde person with a Scandinavian accent, the propositions put forward by all three could be taken to be even more coherent.

However, if we consider just one person who does not integrate new input but merely draws conclusions from what she already believes, the above inequalities seem to amount to a 'cut-prize offer'. For they allow one to increase the coherence of one's doxastic system too simply, viz., just by inferring trivial consequences.[2] Just imagine a physicist arguing as follows: 'I concede that the General Theory of Relativity and the theory of Quantum Mechanics do not really fit together. But we could, effortlessly and without committing ourselves to anything beyond what we are already committed to, weaken the incoherence, merely by adding the conjunction or the disjunction of these theories. And if we do both, our system is in an even better shape.' This is obviously ridiculous. In order to obtain more coherence, our physicist has to try a bit harder.[3]

2. OLSSON'S MEASURE

Olsson (2002, p. 250) tentatively suggests a function quite similar to Shogenji's:

$$C_O(A_1, \ldots, A_n) = \frac{P(A_1 \ldots A_n)}{P(A_1 \vee \cdots \vee A_n)}$$

The idea here is: the closer the probability of *each* proposition being true is to the probability that *at least one* of them is true, the more they cohere. The values of this function range from 0 to 1, making clear at least that 0 represents maximal incoherence and 1 maximal coherence. There is no universal threshold, however, where incoherence passes into coherence. In particular, a value above (below) 0.5 must not be interpreted as meaning that the set is coherent (incoherent).

Although the lack of a neutral point is irrelevant to the following objections, it ensures that Olsson's measure is immune to the problem *subcontraries* pose for Shogenji's account. Remember the murder example. Since one of the statements must be true, $P(M1 \vee M2) = 1$ and thus $C_O(M1, M2) = P(M1 \& M2) = 0.6$. But just as this does not mean that these propositions are incoherent, so it does not mean they fit together. It merely shows that they are neither incoherent nor coherent *to the extreme*.

Moreover, in contrast to Shogenji's formula, Olsson's rules that adding the conjunction or disjunction of the statements in question does not affect coherence. $A \vee B \vee (A\ B)$, as well as $A \vee B \vee (A \vee B)$, are equivalent to $A \vee B$. Hence:

$$C_O(A, B, A\ B) = C_O(A, B, A \vee B) = \frac{P(A\ B)}{P(A \vee B)} = C_O(A, B)$$

However, including a *necessary truth* has the unwanted consequence of rendering the set less coherent (given that $P(A \vee B) < 1$). Since a disjunction of any proposition with a necessity N must be true, we get:

$$C_O(A, B, N) = \frac{P(A\ B\ N)}{P(A \vee B \vee N)} = P(A\ B) < \frac{P(A\ B)}{P(A \vee B)}$$
$$= C_O(A, B)$$

But what about *mathematical truths*? I presume Olsson does not want to say that, in order to stay as coherent as possible, we should avoid assimilating them to our belief system. Shogenji's account is doing better in this respect:

$$C_S(A, B, N) = \frac{P(A\ B\ N)}{P(A) \times P(B) \times P(N)} = \frac{P(A\ B)}{P(A) \times P(B)} = C_S(A, B)$$

As to contrary systems of assumptions, Olsson's measure, just as Shogenji's, cuts a bad figure. If A implies $\neg B$, then $C_O(A, B) = 0$. Hence, such sets would, without exception, be incoherent to the highest extent. But the second power source example (V4–V6) indicates that this is not true. Because of differences in the proximity of numerical values, contrary propositions may display different degrees of incoherence.

Furthermore, if both B and C are logical consequences of A, and if the probability of B does not differ from that of C, Olsson's formula rules that $\{A, B\}$ is coherent to the same extent as $\{A, C\}$. The disjunctions $A \vee B$ and $A \vee C$ are then equivalent to B and C, respectively. Therefore:

$$C_O(A, B) = \frac{P(A\ B)}{P(A \vee B)} = \frac{P(A)}{P(B)} = \frac{P(A)}{P(C)} = \frac{P(A\ C)}{P(A \vee C)} = C_O(A, C)$$

The first example of the power source (V1–V3) makes clear that this is a mistake.[4]

3. FITELSON'S MEASURE

In his article 'A Probabilistic Theory of Coherence' (2003), Fitelson offered a formula which he revised a bit in his online-paper 'Two Technical Corrections to My Coherence Measure' (2004). The starting point of his account is the idea that the degree of coherence depends on the degree of *support* the propositions provide for each other.[5] As to support, aka confirmation, Fitelson adopts Kemeny and Oppenheim's (1952) measure with a slight modification. If B implies A (and is not logically false), then he takes B to confirm A to the maximum degree: $F(A, B) = 1$. If B implies $\neg A$, the support is as small as it can be: $F(A, B) = -1$.[6] And if neither A nor its negation follow from B, the degree of confirmation arises from Kemeny and Oppenheim's original function:

$$F(A, B) = \frac{P(B|A) - P(B|\neg A)}{P(B|A) + P(B|\neg A)}$$

Given the required probabilities, we can calculate the extent to which each proposition in a set, and each conjunction of propositions, is supported by each remaining proposition and each conjunction of them. For example, for a trio of propositions we get 12 such numbers: $F(A, B)$, $F(A, C)$, $F(B, A)$, $F(B, C)$, $F(C, A)$, $F(C, B)$, $F(A, B \& C)$, $F(B, A \& C)$, $F(C, A \& B)$, $F(A \& B, C)$, $F(A \& C, B)$ and $F(B \& C, A)$. The degree of coherence is then defined as the straight average of these values, i.e., their sum divided by their number. Intuitively, coherence is thus identified with average confirmation. Like the values of the support function F, the numbers provided by this measure range from −1 to 1. A value above 0 means that the set is coherent, a value below 0 that it is incoherent.

Despite the initial appeal of Fitelson's recipe, it also produces counter-intuitive results. The first point is that the murder example proves as problematic for Fitelson as it does for Shogenji. Assume, again, that there are ten equiprobable suspects for a murder, where two previously committed a robbery, two pickpocketing and six both crimes. Owing to the sizeable overlap, the pair consisting of

(M1)   The murderer committed a robbery.
(M2)   The murderer committed pickpocketing.

does not seem to be incoherent. However, since each suspect was involved either in a robbery or in pickpocketing, ¬M1 implies M2.

Therefore, $P(M2|\neg M1)$ and $P(M1|\neg M2)$ are both equal to 1, which entails:

$$C_F(M1, M2) = \left(\frac{6/8 - 1}{6/8 + 1} + \frac{6/8 - 1}{6/8 + 1} \right) / 2 < 0$$

Thus, Fitelson's measure leads to the claim that these propositions do not fit together.

This is only one instance of a general problem. Fitelson's measure is unable to cope with subcontraries because it does not allow them to be coherent, only neutral at most. For if $\neg A$ implies B, then:

$$P(A|B) - P(A|\neg B) = P(A|B) - 1 \leq 0$$
$$P(B|A) - P(B|\neg A) = P(B|A) - 1 \leq 0$$

And this means that $C_F(A, B)$ does not exceed the threshold 0 above which coherence begins.[7]

The second point is related to the previous one. There is a simple way to convert any set of propositions into a system of which one statement must be true: just add a necessary truth. Hence, it should come as no surprise that Fitelson's measure has a consequence which resembles one of the deficiencies of Olsson's formula: by assimilating a necessity N to a pair of propositions which support each other to a sufficiently high degree, one *lowers* coherence. If none of the assumptions A or B implies the other one or its negation, $C_F(A, B, N)$ is given by dividing the sum of the following values by 12:

$$F(A, B) = \frac{P(B|A) - P(B|\neg A)}{P(B|A) + P(B|\neg A)}$$

$$F(A, N) = \frac{P(N|A) - P(N|\neg A)}{P(N|A) + P(N|\neg A)} = \frac{1 - 1}{1 + 1} = 0$$

$$F(B, A) = \frac{P(A|B) - P(A|\neg B)}{P(A|B) + P(A|\neg B)}$$

$$F(B, N) = \frac{P(N|B) - P(N|\neg B)}{P(N|B) + P(N|\neg B)} = 0$$

$$F(N, A) = 1 \,(\text{because } N \text{ is implied by any proposition})$$

$$F(N, B) = 1$$

$$F(A, B\ N) = \frac{P(B\ N|A) - P(B\ N|\neg A)}{P(B\ N|A) + P(B\ N|\neg A)} = F(A, B)$$

$$F(B, A\ N) = \frac{P(A\ N|B) - P(A\ N|\neg B)}{P(A\ N|B) + P(A\ N|\neg B)} = F(B, A)$$

$$F(N, A\ B) = 1$$

$$F(A\ B, N) = \frac{P(N|A\ B) - P(N|\neg(A\ B))}{P(N|A\ B) + P(N|\neg(A\ B))} = 0$$

$$F(A\ N, B) = \frac{P(B|A\ N) - P(B|\neg(A\ N))}{P(B|A\ N) + P(B|\neg(A\ N))} = F(A, B)$$

$$F(B\ N, A) = \frac{P(A|B\ N) - P(A|\neg(B\ N))}{P(A|B\ N) + P(A|\neg(B\ N))} = F(B, A)$$

Now suppose that A and B confirm each other to such a degree that $F(A, B) + F(B, A) > 1$. Then:

$$C_F(A, B, N) = [3 \times F(A, B) + 3 \times F(B, A) + 3 \times 1 + 3 \times 0]/12$$
$$< [6 \times F(A, B) + 6 \times F(B, A)]/12 = C_F(A, B)$$

This is surprising in itself; but what is even more surprising is that it is possible to obtain the opposite result as well, namely if $F(A, B) + F(B, A)$ is smaller than 1. That is, the impact of necessities would depend on how much A and B support each other. This is a behaviour for which I see no good reason.

Note that I do not call into question the intuitive idea underlying Fitelson's proposal. The above-mentioned difficulties do not originate from the fact that he wants to capture coherence in terms of *confirmation*; they are rather due to his wish to get a grip on coherence by relying on nothing but *probability*. For in order to construct a measure of coherence which is both probabilistic and sensitive to confirmation, he has to make use of a probabilistic account of confirmation. It is this translation into the language of probability that is causing the problem.

There is disagreement among advocates of probabilistic epistemology on the quantitative question of how to measure the degree to which B supports A. Some rely on the difference $P(A|B) - P(A)$, others prefer the ratio $P(A|B)/P(A)$ or a logarithm thereof, Fitelson adopts Kemeny and Oppenheim's function, and there are further proposals.[8] But when it comes to the qualitative question under which conditions B provides any confirmation for A at all, they unanimously rely on the so-called relevance criterion:

B confirms A iff $P(A|B) > P(A)$; B disconfirms A iff

$P(A|B) < P(A)$; and B is confirmationally irrelevant to A

iff $P(A|B) = P(A)$[9]

From this principle, we are allowed to infer that B undermines A if it is implied by its negation (provided B does not have a prior probability of 1). For then $P(\neg A \ \& \ B) = P(\neg A)$ so that:

$$P(A|B) = 1 - P(\neg A|B) = 1 - \frac{P(\neg A \ B)}{P(B)} = 1 - \frac{P(\neg A)}{P(B)}$$

$$< 1 - P(\neg A) = P(A)$$

A proponent of the relevance criterion is thus committed to the claim that evidence cannot speak in favour of a hypothesis if they are subcontraries. This result in itself might already arouse some suspicion. Instead of jumping to conclusions, however, let us see what happens if it is considered in connection with the starting point of Fitelson's measure of coherence.

Fitelson assumes that coherence is sensitive to support. This is perfectly reasonable. If we look at how scientists conceive of confirmation and coherence, a particular connection between them is quite obvious: a hypothesis fits the experimental data only if they support it. Or put the other way round, if the data disconfirm the hypothesis, it does not cohere with them. Assume a chemist carries out an experiment on Boyle's Law, which states that, at a constant temperature, the pressure of a given quantity of gas is inversely proportional to its volume. Before the chemist reduces the volume of the gas by half, the barometer measures a pressure of 1 bar; afterwards its reading is 3 bars. Since Boyle's Law predicts 2 bars, the chemist will thus take her experimental result to undermine the former (if she thinks that the barometer is reliable), inferring from this that Boyle's Law does not dovetail with her observation. Thus, scientifically pertinent conceptions of confirmation and coherence should respect the following bridge principle:

If B disconfirms A, then $\{A, B\}$ is incoherent.

The relevance criterion, however, entails that B speaks against A if one of them must be true and $P(B)$ is smaller than 1. Hence, together with the bridge principle, it rules:

If A and B are subcontraries and $P(B) < 1$,

then $\{A, B\}$ is incoherent.

But the murder example (M1–M2) indicates that this is questionable. The given propositions are subcontraries with a probability below 1. Nevertheless, they appear to fit together.

The moral here is that the relevance criterion is dubious. It is therefore no wonder that a measure of coherence based on it will run into problems. As mentioned, the reason for the inadequate treatment of subcontrary propositions does not lie in Fitelson's idea that coherence can be spelled out in terms of confirmation. The bridge principle makes clear that these notions are indeed connected. Rather, the problem lies in Fitelson's probabilistic orientation, i.e., his presumption that confirmation, and thereby coherence, can be given a purely probabilistic shape.

A third problem is that Fitelson's measure agrees with Shogenji's in permitting the coherence to be increased by adding the conjunction of the propositions at issue. Consider the following distribution:

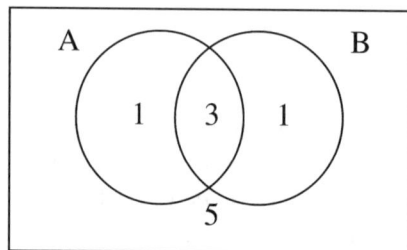

Since this distribution is symmetrical, and since A & B implies both A and B and is implied by A and B together:

$$F(A, B) = F(B, A) = \frac{3/4 - 1/6}{3/4 + 1/6} \approx 0.64$$

$$F(A, (A\ B)) = F(B, (A\ B)) = F(A, B\ (A\ B))$$
$$= F(B, A\ (A\ B)) = F((A\ B), A\ B)$$
$$= F(A\ B, (A\ B)) = 1$$

$$F((A\ B), A) = F((A\ B), B) = F(A\ (A\ B), B)$$
$$= F(B\ (A\ B), A) = \frac{1 - 1/7}{1 + 1/7} = 0.75$$

Hence:

$$C_F(A, B, A\ B) \approx [2 \times 0.64 + 6 \times 1 + 4 \times 0.75]/12 \approx 0.86$$
$$> [2 \times 0.64]/2 = 0.64 \approx C_F(A, B)$$

The same happens when we add the disjunction $A \lor B$. Since both A and B entail it, and since we have a symmetrical distribution:

$$F(A, B) = F(A, B\ (A \vee B)) = F(A\ (A \vee B), B) = F(B, A)$$
$$= F(B, A\ (A \vee B)) = F(B\ (A \vee B), A) \approx 0.64$$

$$F(A \vee B, A) = F(A \vee B, B) = F(A \vee B, A\ B) = 1$$

$$F(A, A \vee B) = F(B, A \vee B) = \frac{1 - 1/6}{1 + 1/6} \approx 0.71$$

$$F(A\ B, A \vee B) = \frac{1 - 2/7}{1 + 2/7} \approx 0.56$$

And so:

$$C_F(A, B, A \vee B) \approx [6 \times 0.64 + 3 \times 1 + 2 \times 0.71 + 0.56]/12$$
$$\approx 0.74 > [2 \times 0.64]/2 = 0.64 \approx C_F(A, B)$$

As already stated in connection with Shogenji's proposal, this would mean that the coherence of a system can be improved simply by drawing trivial conclusions.

Fourth, Fitelson's measure fares no better than Shogenji's and Olsson's when we look at pairs of contrary statements. If A and B exclude each other, both $F(A, B)$ and $F(B, A)$ are -1, which entails that $C_F(A, B)$ is also -1. That is, Fitelson's formula puts on a par all two-member systems of inconsistent assumptions, namely as being incoherent to the highest degree. But remember the example of the physicist who wants to know the voltage of a power source. The prior probability of that voltage being 2 V is identical with the prior probability of its being 50 V. She asks her assistants, and their answers are:

(V4)   The voltage is 1 V.
(V5)   The voltage is 2 V.
(V6)   The voltage is 50 V.

{V4, V5} is less incoherent than {V4, V6} because 1 V is closer to 2 V than to 50 V.

Fifth, as an advantage of his measure over Shogenji's, Fitelson (2003, p. 179) points out that, if A implies B, the degree of coherence depends not only on the probability of B but also on the statistical relationship between A and B:

348 MARK SIEBEL

$$C_F(A, B) = \left(\frac{1 - P(B|\neg A)}{1 + P(B|\neg A)} + \frac{P(A|B) - 0}{P(A|B) + 0}\right)/2$$
$$= \left(\frac{1 - P(B|\neg A)}{1 + P(B|\neg A)} + \frac{1 + P(B|\neg A)}{1 + P(B|\neg A)}\right)/2 = \frac{1}{1 + P(B|\neg A)}$$

Although it might be reasonable to let the relationship between A and B play a role here, I do not believe that Fitelson's specific account is on the right track. Take the other power source example, where a voltage of 2 V is again as probable as a voltage of 50 V:

(V1)   The voltage is 1 V.
(V2)   The voltage is 1 or 2 V.
(V3)   The voltage is 1 or 50 V.

Fitelson is obliged to claim that these pairs possess the same coherence. Since both $\neg V2$ and $\neg V3$ imply $\neg V1$, $P(\neg V1|\neg V2) = P(\neg V1|\neg V3) = 1$. Hence, since $P(\neg V2) = P(\neg V3)$:

$$C_F(V1, V2) = \frac{1}{1 + 1 - P(\neg V2|\neg V1)} = \frac{1}{2 - P(\neg V2) \times \frac{P(\neg V1|\neg V2)}{P(\neg V1)}}$$
$$= \frac{1}{2 - \frac{P(\neg V2)}{P(\neg V1)}} = \frac{1}{2 - \frac{P(\neg V3)}{P(\neg V1)}} = C_F(V1, V3)$$

But {V1, V2} is endowed with a greater coherence than {V1, V3} because V2's alternative to V1 is numerically closer to V1 than V3's alternative.[10]

4. DOUVEN AND MEIJS'S MEASURE

Douven and Meijs's (2006, sect. 3) proposal is quite similar to Fitelson's. They diverge merely in terms of choosing the difference measure of confirmation instead of (a modified variant of) Kemeny and Oppenheim's formula. Thus, they take the coherence of a two-member set as given by:

$$C_{DM}(A, B) = [P(A|B) - P(A) + P(B|A) - P(B)]/2$$

The values of this function range from −1 to 1. Douven and Meijs do not explicitly distinguish a threshold above which coherence begins. But their account suggests that, like Fitelson, they have 0 in

[56]

mind. For it appears that they consider pairs of propositions which neither support nor undermine each other to be neither coherent nor incoherent. Now, in terms of the relevance criterion, A and B are confirmationally irrelevant to each other just in case $P(A|B) = P(A)$, which entails that $P(B|A) = P(B)$. But then $P(A|B) - P(A) = P(B|A) - P(B) = 0$; and thus $C_{DM}(A, B)$ is also 0. It is therefore reasonable to assume that Douven and Meijs interpret a value of 0 as meaning that the pair is neither coherent nor incoherent. Analogously, if there is mutual disconfirmation between the propositions – viz., $P(A|B) < P(A)$ so that also $P(B|A) < P(B)$ – then $C_{DM}(A, B) < 0$, suggesting that a value smaller than 0 stands for incoherence.

It should be noted that Douven and Meijs (2006, sect. 5.1) restrict their measure to sets of propositions which are pairwise logically independent. Thereby they immunise it against a number of objections, including the ones following below. However, since such a scope restriction, in view of counter-examples, smacks of an 'easy way out', I take the liberty of presenting some consequences of the unqualified variant of their proposal.

The first difficulty is that adding a necessity would *decrease* coherence. For $C_{DM}(A, B, N)$ is identical with

$$
\begin{aligned}
&[P(A|B) - P(A) + P(A|N) - P(A) + P(B|A) - P(B) + P(B|N) \\
&\quad - P(B) + P(N|A) - P(N) + P(N|B) - P(N) + P(A|B\ N) \\
&\quad - P(A) + P(B|A\ N) - P(B) + P(N|A\ B) - P(N) \\
&\quad + P(A\ B|N) - P(A\ B) + P(A\ N|B) - P(A\ N) \\
&\quad + P(B\ N|A) - P(B\ N)]/12
\end{aligned}
$$

But this reduces to

$$
3 \times [P(A|B) - P(A) + P(B|A) - P(B)]/12,
$$

which is obviously smaller than

$$
[P(A|B) - P(A) + P(B|A) - P(B)]/2
$$

Second, by including the conjunction or disjunction of A and B, we could easily *increase* coherence. By taking the distribution used as a test case for Fitelson's measure, we get $C_{DM}(A, B) = 0.35$, $C_{DM}(A, B, A\ B) \approx 0.53$ and $C_{DM}(A, B, A \vee B) \approx 0.39$. (I spare the reader the calculations.)

Third and fourth, {A, B} and {A, C} would be (in)coherent to the same degree if A implies the equiprobable statements B and C or their negations. In the former case:

$$C_{DM}(A,B) = [P(A) \times P(B|A)/P(B) - P(A) + P(B|A) - P(B)]/2$$
$$= [P(A)/P(C) - P(A) + 1 - P(C)]/2 = C_{DM}(A,C)$$

In the latter case:

$$C_{DM}(A,B) = [0 - P(A) + 0 - P(B)]/2$$
$$= [0 - P(A) + 0 - P(C)]/2 = C_{DM}(A,C)$$

The power source examples (V1–V3) and (V4–V6) speak against these equations.

The fifth and final difficulty of Douven and Meijs's measure is that pairs of subcontrary propositions would not fit together, even if there was a high amount of overlap. For if $\neg A$ entails B, $P(A|B) < P(A)$ and $P(B|A) < P(B)$ so that $C_{DM}(A,B) < 0$. But recall the murder example (M1–M2).

5. BOVENS AND HARTMANN'S QUASI-ORDERING

Although the main topic of this paper is probabilistic *measures* of coherence, I do not want to ignore Bovens and Hartmann's *quasi-ordering*. In their book *Bayesian Epistemology* (2003b, chs. 1f.), they argue that the following function enables us to determine the relative coherence of two sets of propositions (see also Bovens and Hartmann 2003a, Sects. 4f.):

$$C_r(A_1, \ldots A_n) = \frac{a_0 + (1 - a_0)(1 - r)^n}{\sum_{i=0}^{n} a_i (1 - r)^i},$$

where a_i is the probability that i of the n statements are false, and r is the reliability of the statements' sources. (The sources are supposed to be independent in a specific way; and they are partially reliable such that, on the definition of r, $0 < r < 1$.) To be sure, C_r does not represent the propositions' degree of coherence because it is functionally dependent on the credibility of their sources. Bovens and Hartmann's claim is rather that supplementing this formula with a simple assumption makes it possible to compare systems of statements with respect to coherence:

S_1 is at least as coherent as S_2 iff for all values of r, $C_r(S_1)$ $\geq C_r(S_2)$.

Thus, if the C_r-values for S_1 are, for all degrees of partial reliability, always greater (smaller) than the corresponding values for S_2, then S_1 is more (less) coherent than S_2.

Bovens and Hartmann present a number of examples in order to show that their model is in a better position than those of Shogenji, Olsson and Fitelson. As far as these examples are concerned, this is true. However, they did not examine what happens when a necessary truth N is added to a system of propositions. Let a_i be the probability that i statements in the two-member set $\{A, B\}$ are false, and b_i the probability that i propositions in the extended set $\{A, B, N\}$ are false. Then:

$$b_0 = P(A\ B\ N) = P(A\ B) = a_0$$
$$b_1 = P(A\ B\ \neg N) + P(A\ \neg B\ N) + P(\neg A\ B\ N)$$
$$= P(A\ \neg B) + P(\neg A\ B) = a_1$$
$$b_2 = P(A\ \neg B\ \neg N) + P(\neg A\ \neg B\ N) + P(\neg A\ B\ \neg N)$$
$$= P(\neg A\ \neg B) = a_2$$
$$b_3 = P(\neg A\ \neg B\ \neg N) = 0$$

Therefore, $C_r(A, B, N)$ reads:

$$\frac{b_0 + (1 - b_0)(1 - r)^3}{b_0 + b_1(1 - r) + b_2(1 - r)^2 + b_3(1 - r)^3}$$
$$= \frac{a_0 + (1 - a_0)(1 - r)^3}{a_0 + a_1(1 - r) + a_2(1 - r)^2},$$

while $C_r(A, B)$ is:

$$\frac{a_0 + (1 - a_0)(1 - r)^2}{a_0 + a_1(1 - r) + a_2(1 - r)^2}$$

The denominators of these fractions are identical. Since $0 < (1-r) < 1$, $(1-r)^3 < (1-r)^2$. Hence, if a_0, i.e., $P(A\ B)$, is smaller than 1 (which it usually will be), then $C_r(A, B, N)$ is smaller than $C_r(A, B)$ for all values of the reliability parameter r. This means, according to Bovens and Hartmann's proposal, that enriching a pair of such statements with a necessary truth lowers coherence. Their model is thus subject to the same difficulty as Olsson's. It is hardly acceptable that learning a truth of mathematics makes one's doxastic system less coherent.

Second, like Shogenji's account, Bovens and Hartmann's entails that assimilating the conjunction of two propositions is a reasonable method for increasing coherence. Again, a_i stands for the probability that i statements from pair $\{A, B\}$ are false, while b_i is the probability that i propositions in the extended set $\{A, B, A \ \& \ B\}$ are false. Then:

$$b_0 = P(A \ B \ (A \ B)) = P(A \ B) = a_0$$
$$b_1 = P(A \ B \ \neg(A \ B)) + P(A \ \neg B \ (A \ B))$$
$$\qquad + P(\neg A \ B \ (A \ B)) = 0$$
$$b_2 = P(A \ \neg B \ \neg(A \ B)) + P(\neg A \ \neg B \ (A \ B))$$
$$\qquad + P(\neg A \ B \ \neg(A \ B)) = P(A \ \neg B)$$
$$\qquad + P(\neg A \ B) = a_1$$
$$b_3 = P(\neg A \ \neg B \ \neg(A \ B)) = P(\neg A \ \neg B) = a_2$$

Since $1 - a_0 = a_1 + a_2$, this entails:

$$C_r(A, B, A \ B) = \frac{b_0 + (1 - b_0)(1 - r)^3}{b_0 + b_1(1 - r) + b_2(1 - r)^2 + b_3(1 - r)^3}$$
$$= \frac{a_0 + a_1(1 - r)^3 + a_2(1 - r)^3}{a_0 + a_1(1 - r)^2 + a_2(1 - r)^3},$$

While

$$C_r(A, B) = \frac{a_0 + a_1(1 - r)^2 + a_2(1 - r)^2}{a_0 + a_1(1 - r) + a_2(1 - r)_2}$$

$C_r(A, B, A\&B)$ is greater than $C_r(A, B)$ if $\frac{C_r(A,B,A \ \& \ B)}{C_r(A,B)} > 1$, that is, if

$$\left[a_0 + a_1(1 - r)^2 + a_2(1 - r)^3 \right] \times \left[a_0 + a_1(1 - r)^2 + a_2(1 - r)^2 \right]$$

is greater than

$$\left[a_0 + a_1(1 - r)^2 + a_2(1 - r)^3 \right] \times \left[a_0 + a_1(1 - r)^2 + a_2(1 - r)^2 \right]$$

The former is

$$a_0^2 + \underline{a_0 a_1(1 - r)} + a_0 a_2(1 - r)^2 + \underline{a_0 a_1(1 - r)^3} + a_1^2(1 - r)^4$$
$$+ a_1 a_2(1 - r)^5 + a_0 a_2(1 - r)^3 + a_1 a_2(1 - r)^4 + a_2^2(1 - r)^5$$

The latter is

$$a_0^2 + \underline{a_0 a_1(1 - r)^2} + a_0 a_2(1 - r)^2 + \underline{a_0 a_1(1 - r)^2} + a_1^2(1 - r)^4$$
$$+ a_1 a_2(1 - r)^4 + a_0 a_2(1 - r)^3 + a_1 a_2(1 - r)^5 + a_2^2(1 - r)^5$$

Since these sums differ only in the underlined addends, the former is greater than the latter if

$$(1-r) + (1-r)^3 - (1-r)^2 - (1-r)^2 > 0$$

The left hand side of this equation is identical with

$$[(1-r)^2 - (1-r)] \times [(1-r) - 1]$$

Since $0 < (1-r) < 1$, $(1-r)^2 < (1-r) < 1$, so that both of these multiplicands are negative and their product is positive. Therefore, if neither a_0 nor a_1 is 0, i.e., $A \& B, A \& \neg B$ and $\neg A \& B$ do not have zero probability, then $C_r(A, B, A \& B) > C_r(A, B)$ for all values of the reliability parameter r.

An analogous derivation shows that Bovens and Hartmann's proposal amounts to the claim that adding the *disjunction* of two propositions makes the system *less* coherent. They should then approve of the following instruction: if you are interested in maximising coherence, infer from two propositions that their con-junction is true, but do not infer that at least one of them is true. I cannot see any justification for taking that stance. Third, like all the other models, Bovens and Hartmann's does not properly capture the power source example (V1–V3). If both B and C follow from A, and if these consequences possess the same probability, then:

$$P(A\ B) = P(A) = P(A\ C)$$
$$P(A\ \neg B) = 0 = P(A\ \neg C)$$
$$P(\neg A\ B) = P(\neg(A \lor \neg B)) = 1 - P(A \lor \neg B)$$
$$= 1 - (P(A) + P(\neg C)) = P(\neg A\ C)$$
$$P(\neg A\ \neg B) = P(\neg B) = P(\neg C) = P(\neg A\ \neg C)$$

Therefore:

$$C_r(A, B) = \frac{P(A) + (1 - P(A))(1 - r)^2}{P(A) + P(\neg A\ B)(1 - r) + P(\neg B)(1 - r)^2}$$

$$= \frac{P(A) + (1 - P(A))(1 - r)^2}{P(A) + P(\neg A\ C)(1 - r) + P(\neg C)(1 - r)^2} = C_r(A, C)$$

That is, in the light of Bovens and Hartmann's account, pairs of this fashion cannot differ in coherence. Due to the greater proximity of the numerical values, however, 'The voltage is 1 V' fits 'The voltage is 1 or 2 V' more than 'The voltage is 1 or 50 V', even if the latter propositions are equally likely.

A similar problem arises in the case of contrary statements. If A implies both $\neg B$ and $\neg C$, and if $P(B) = P(C)$, then it follows:

$$P(A\ B) = 0 = P(A\ C)$$
$$P(A\ \neg B) = P(A) = P(A\ \neg C)$$
$$P(\neg A\ B) = P(B) = P(C) = P(\neg A\ C)$$
$$P(\neg A\ \neg B) = P(\neg(A \vee B)) = 1 - P(A \vee B)$$
$$= 1 - (P(A) + P(B)) = 1 - (P(A) + P(C))$$
$$= P(\neg A\ \neg C)$$

And thus:

$$C_r(A,B) = \frac{(1-r)^2}{(P(A)+P(B))(1-r)+P(\neg A\ \neg B)(1-r)^2}$$
$$= \frac{(1-r)^2}{(P(A)+P(C))(1-r)+P(\neg A\ \neg C)(1-r)^2}$$
$$= C_r(A,C)$$

But look at the example (V4–V6). Although neither 'The voltage is 1 V' and 'The voltage is 2 V' nor the former and 'The voltage is 50 V' fit together, the incoherence is weaker in the former case because 2 V is closer to 1 V.

6. SUMMARY OF THE OBJECTIONS

The following table summarises the objections presented in the previous sections. A minus sign means that the case at hand causes difficulties for the corresponding account while a plus sign means that it is adequately handled. Two boxes must be left empty. Neither

	Contrary propositions (V4–V6)	Subcontrary propositions (M1–M2)	Conjunctions and disjunctions	Logical consequences (V1–V3)	Necessary truths
Shogenji	–	–	–	–	+
Olsson	–		+	–	–
Fitelson	–	–	–	–	–
Douven & Meijs	–	–	–	–	–
Bovens & Hartmann	–		–	–	–

Olsson's nor Bovens and Hartmann's theories state that subcontrary propositions do not dovetail. The reason is, however, that their formulae are not connected with a specification of a numerical range standing for incoherence. I therefore deem a plus sign as misleading as a minus sign.

Regarding the inclusion of the conjunction or disjunction of two statements, I consider a *change* in coherence as problematic because, if a person just infers such a proposition from what she already believes, this does not seem to have an influence on the coherence of her doxastic system. Remember, however, that there are other cases where an increase in coherence can be attested. For example, let two witnesses report *A* and *B*, respectively, and then a third one *A* & *B*. Since intuitions vary, depending on the origins of the statements in question,[11] I do not wish to overemphasise this issue. None of the measures under consideration can do justice to *both* types of cases because they treat them in a uniform way, regardless of whether the conjunction was put forward by a further witness or merely inferred by someone from what she already accepted. But note also that this is no excuse for the behaviour of Bovens and Hartmann's quasi-ordering, according to which the conjunction *raises* coherence whereas the disjunction *lowers* it.

7. GENERAL OBJECTIONS

It has been argued that none of the probabilistic measures of coherence that have been put on the market withstands close scrutiny. This is, of course, far from proving that it is *impossible* to construct such a measure. 'Shogenji, Olsson, Fitelson, and Douven and Meijs went wrong, to be sure; but let us wait and see what the future holds in store', so one might think.

But note that some of the objections apply to *all* proposals. Among other things, none of them has been able to deal with the power source example (V1--V3). The downside is that this problem generalises. *Any* probabilistic measure, whatever it looks like in detail, has to assign the same degree of coherence to {*A, B*} and {*A, C*} if both *B* and *C* are logical consequences of *A*, and if these consequences possess the same probability. But this is not tenable because such pairs may very well differ in the degree to which they fit together.

A probabilistic measure consists in a function whose arguments are tuples of probabilities relating to the propositions in question.

For the two-member case $\{A, B\}$, these tuples might contain $P(A)$, $P(\neg B)$, $P(A \& B)$, $P(A \lor B)$, $P(A|B)$, $P(B|\neg A)$, and so on. Moreover, a function is an *unambiguous* relation. That is, by using the same argument, we obtain the same value. The problem then is: if a proposition A implies both B and C, and if $P(B) = P(C)$, then each and every probability relating to A and B is identical with the corresponding probability involving A and C. For the joint probability distributions for these sets of propositions will be identical.

Such distributions specify the probability of each possible combination of values for the given variables. In the case of a pair of statements, whose values are *true* and *false*, they determine the probabilities of $A \& B$, $A \& \neg B$, $\neg A \& B$ and $\neg A \& \neg B$. Moreover, given a joint probability distribution, any further probability about the domain is fixed because it can be calculated from the distribution.

Now, in connection with Bovens and Hartmann's quasi-ordering, we have seen already that, if B and C are equiprobable consequences of A, then $P(A \& B) = P(A \& C)$, $P(A \neg B) = P(A \neg C)$, $P(\neg A B) = P(\neg A C)$ and $P(\neg A \neg B) = P(\neg A \neg C)$. That is, the joint probability distributions for $\{A, B\}$ and $\{A, C\}$ are the same, entailing that there is no difference between the probabilities belonging to $\{A, B\}$ and the corresponding probabilities relating to $\{A, C\}$. Hence, in such a case the tuples entering our probabilistic coherence function are *identical, no matter which tuples of probabilities the function takes as arguments*. And since a function provides identical values for identical arguments, it will assign these sets the same coherence value. Consequently, probabilistic measures are not able to differentiate finely enough. After all, the power source example (V1--V3) has shown that there are cases of this type where differences in the proximity of numerical values lead to differences in coherence.

The same holds for contrary statements. In the section on Bovens and Hartmann's approach, it was also pointed out that the joint probability distributions for $\{A, B\}$ and $\{A, C\}$ are identical if A implies both $\neg B$ and $\neg C$ and if $P(B) = P(C)$. Thus, a probabilistic coherence function must necessarily turn out the same value for such pairs. But consider example (V4--V6). Even if a voltage of 2 V is as likely as a voltage of 50 V, I presume that a physicist would take the former to be less in disharmony with 'The power source has a voltage of 1 V' than the latter. If one puts on one's 'probabilistic glasses', one will not see this difference because they are too weak.

Aside from these direct arguments, there is a more indirect one. Laurence BonJour (1985, p. 98) has emphasised that "the coherence of a system [...] is enhanced by the presence of *explanatory* relations between its members".[12] The more of them can be established and the better the explanations are, the more the propositions fit together. For example, if hypothesis H_1 makes for an explanation for the data D_1 and D_2, whereas H_2 explains only D_1, then $\{H_1, D_1, D_2\}$ is, ceteris paribus, more coherent than $\{H_2, D_1, D_2\}$. And if H_1 explains D_1 better than D_2, then $\{H_1, D_1\}$ is, ceteris paribus, more coherent than $\{H_1, D_2\}$.

The crucial point then is that a proper theory of coherence must take such principles into account. That is, in order to gain control over *coherence* with probabilistic means, it is required that *explanation* be captured solely in terms of probability. But the proposals put forward so far give little cause for hope.

It is well known that Hempel's (1965) DN/IS model, according to which, roughly, H explains D if P(D|H) is close to 1, has failed. It is highly likely that Tom will not become pregnant, given that he regularly takes birth control pills; but this fact does not explain the former. Neither does Salmon's (1970) idea work, which is, again roughly, that H explains D if $P(D|H) > P(H)$ and H is not screened off from D by other putative explanantia. One of Achinstein's (1983, p. 168) counter-examples to Hempel's account proves that this is wrong. Suppose Susan swallows a pound of arsenic in order to commit suicide. Shortly after, however, she dies because she is run over by a bus. Then it is the collision with the bus, and not the arsenic, which explains her death. But let us assume that, in contrast to swallowing a pound of arsenic, such a collision does not always lead to death. Then $P(\text{death}|\text{arsenic}) > P(\text{death})$, and the collision does not screen off ingestion of arsenic from death because $P(\text{death}|\text{bus \& arsenic})$ is not identical with, but higher than, $P(\text{death}|\text{bus})$. Salmon's account thus rules that Susan's death can be explained by her swallowing arsenic.

'But', one may reply, 'this merely shows that Hempel and Salmon have failed. Why should we assume that any future account will do no better?' Here is the reason why I believe that this assumption is indeed warranted. Consider the following statements:

(D)   The barometers in Hamburg fall.

(H2)   There is a drop in atmospheric pressure in Hamburg & A drop in atmospheric pressure causes barometers to fall.

(H3)   The barometers in Hamburg fall & (There is a drop in atmospheric pressure in Hamburg ∨ The barometers in Hamburg do not fall) & A drop in atmospheric pressure causes barometers to fall.

Both H2 and H3 entail D. But whereas H2 provides an explanation for D, H3 does not. After all, H3 would not imply D if it did not already include the latter; and an inference which essentially contains its conclusion as a premise can hardly be of explanatory value. One cannot explain an event by itself.

A probabilistic theory, however, will tell us that H3 explains D just as much as H2 does. For H3 is equivalent to H2, and thus $P(\text{H3}) = P(\text{H2})$. Moreover, since D is a consequence of both H2 and H3, $P(\text{D \& H2}) = P(\text{H2})$ and $P(\text{D \& H3}) = P(\text{H3})$. Therefore:

$$P(\text{D H2}) = P(\text{H2}) = P(\text{H3}) = P(\text{D H3})$$

$$P(\text{D } \neg\text{H2}) = P(\neg(\neg\text{D} \vee \text{H2})) = 1 - P(\neg\text{D} \vee \text{H2})$$

$$= 1 - (P(\neg\text{D}) + P(\text{H2})) = 1 - (P(\neg\text{D})$$

$$+ P(\text{H3})) = P(\text{D } \neg\text{H3})$$

$$P(\neg\text{D H2}) = 0 = P(\neg\text{D H3})$$

$$P(\neg\text{D } \neg\text{H2}) = P(\neg\text{D}) = P(\neg\text{D } \neg\text{H3})$$

That is, the joint probability distribution for {D, H2} matches that for {D, H3}, which means that any probability relating to the former pair is identical with the corresponding probability relating to the latter. An account which allows a variation in explanation only if there is a variation in probability is thus not able to honour H2 with explaining D while denying H3 this status. But if probabilistic theories cannot cope with explanation, they will hardly be able to deal with coherence.

My conclusion is therefore that it is not just the specific accounts of coherence discussed here which are on the wrong track. It would rather appear that the whole project should be dismissed because probabilistic measures are not sophisticated enough. Probability might be *one* of the aspects which are crucial to coherence, but coherence is a notion too rich to be captured by *nothing but* probabilistic terms.[13]

ACKNOWLEDGEMENTS

This paper grew out of the project Explanatory Coherence, funded by the *Deutsche Forschungsgemeinschaft*. I would like to thank Adelheid Baker, Thomas Bartelborth, Richard Booth, Luc Bovens, Branden

Fitelson, Wouter Meijs, Luca Moretti, Erik Olsson, Mark Textor and Werner Wolff for many helpful comments on precursors of this contribution or related papers.

NOTES

[1] Lewis's (1946, p. 338) qualitative theory of 'congruence' may be deemed a forerunner of these probabilistic measures.
[2] Cf. Douven and Meijs (2006, sect. 5.1) and Moretti and Akiba (2006, sects. 1f).
[3] For a further objection to Shogenji's measure, see Bovens and Hartmann (2003b, p. 50). Cf. also Siebel and Wolff (2005), where it is shown that his proposal and that of Douven and Meijs do not respect the intuition that equivalent witness reports are highly coherent.
[4] Bovens and Hartmann (2003b, p. 50) point out an additional difficulty.
[5] Although developed independently of Douven and Meijs's (2006, sects. 2f.) recipe for generating probabilistic measures of coherence, Fitelson's proposal follows it.
[6] These additions make sure one obtains maximal values for all of these deductive cases. The Kemeny/Oppenheim measure is undefined if $P(B)$ is 0 or $P(A)$ is 0 or 1.
[7] Cf. Siebel (2004) and, for a similar but more complicated argument, Bovens and Hartmann (2003b, p. 51).
[8] For overviews and the pros and cons of different measures, see Kyburg (1983, sect. IV), Eells and Fitelson (2002) and Fitelson (1999, 2001).
[9] Strictly speaking, the common denominator of probabilistic accounts of confirmation is a slightly qualified variant of the relevance criterion. For Fitelson takes B to support A if A is a logical truth and B not a logical falsehood, although in this case $P(A| B) = P(A)$. But if we restrict the relevance criterion to contingent propositions, all probabilists will agree to it.
[10] See Douven and Meijs (2006, sect. 4), for a further problem with Fitelson's measure.
[11] Cf. Shogenji (2001, p. 149f.) and Moretti and Akiba (2006, sect. 8).
[12] Cf. also Thagard (1992, ch. 4.1) and Bartelborth (1996, sects. IV.D, IV.F).
[13] In Siebel (2005), I make a point in favour of a corrected variant of Thagard's measure (cf. Thagard 1992, ch. 4; Thagard and Verbeurgt 1998, sect. 2).

REFERENCES

Achinstein, P.: 1983, *The Nature of Explanation*, Oxford University Press, New York and Oxford.

Akiba, K.: 2000, 'Shogenji's Probabilistic Measure of Coherence Is Incoherent', *Analysis* **60**, 356–359.

Bartelborth, T.: 1996, *Begründungsstrategien Ein Weg durch die analytische Erkenntnistheorie*, Akademie-Verlag, Berlin.

BonJour, L.: 1985, *The Structure of Empirical Knowledge*, Harvard University Press, Cambridge/Mass. and London.

Bovens, L. and S. Hartmann: 2003a, 'Solving the Riddle of Coherence', *Mind* **112**, 601–633.

Bovens, L. and S. Hartmann: 2003b, *Bayesian Epistemology*, Oxford University Press, New York and Oxford.

Douven, I. and W. Meijs: 2006, 'Measuring Coherence', *Synthese*, to appear.

Eells, E. and B. Fitelson: 2002, 'Symmetries and Asymmetries in Evidential Support', *Philosophical Studies* **107**, 129–142.

Fitelson, B.: 1999, 'The Plurality of Bayesian Measures of Confirmation and the Problem of Measure Sensitivity', *Philosophy of Science* **66** (Proceedings), 362–378.

Fitelson, B.: 2001, *Studies in Bayesian Confirmation Theory*, Ph.D. thesis, University of Wisconsin at Madison. Online: http://fitelson.org/thesis.pdf.

Fitelson, B.: 2003, 'A Probabilistic Theory of Coherence', *Analysis* **63**, 194–199.

Fitelson, B.: 2004, 'Two Technical Corrections to My Coherence Measure', http://fitelson.org/coherence2.pdf.

Hempel, C. G.: 1965, 'Aspects of Scientific Explanation', in *Aspects of Scientific Explanation and Other Essays in the Philosophy of Science*, The Free Press, New York and London, 331–496.

Kemeny, J. and P. Oppenheim: 1952, 'Degrees of Factual Support', *Philosophy of Science* **19**, 307–324.

Kyburg, H. E. Jr.: 1983, 'Recent Work in Inductive Logic', in T. Machan & K. Lucey (eds.), *Recent Work in Philosophy*, Rowman and Allanheld, Totowa/NJ, 87–150.

Lewis, C. I.: 1946, *An Analysis of Knowledge and Valuation*, Open Court, Chicago.

Moretti, L. and K. Akiba: 2006, 'Probabilistic Measures of Coherence and the Problem of Belief Individuation', *Synthese*, to appear.

Olsson, E.: 2002, 'What is the Problem of Coherence and Truth', *The Journal of Philosophy* **94**, 246–272.

Salmon, W. C.: 1970, 'Statistical Explanation', in R. G. Colodny (ed.), *The Nature and Function of Scientific Theories*, University of Pittsburgh Press, Pittsburgh, pp. 173–231.

Shogenji, T.: 1999, 'Is Coherence Truth Conducive?', *Analysis* **59**, 338–345.

Shogenji, T.: 2001, 'Reply to Akiba on the Probabilistic Measure of Coherence', *Analysis* **61**, 147–150.

Siebel, M.: 2004, 'On Fitelson's Measure of Coherence', *Analysis* **64**, 189–190.

Siebel, M.: 2005, 'Thagard's Measure of Coherence: Corrected and Compared with Probabilistic Accounts', submitted to synthese.

Siebel, M. and W. Wolff: 2005, 'Equivalent Testimonies as a Touchstone of Coherence Measures', manuscript.

Thagard, P.: 1992, *Conceptual Revolutions*, Princeton University Press, Princeton.

Thagard, P. and K. Verbeurgt: 1998, 'Coherence as Constraint Satisfaction', *Cognitive Science* **22**, 1–24.

Department of Philosophy,
Univeristy of Hamburg,
Von-Melle-Park 6,
20146 Hamburg,
Germany

Erkenntnis (2005) 63:361–374
DOI 10.1007/s10670-005-4005-1

LUC BOVENS and STEPHAN HARTMANN

WHY THERE CANNOT BE A SINGLE PROBABILISTIC MEASURE OF COHERENCE

ABSTRACT. *Bayesian Coherence Theory of Justification* or, for short, *Bayesian Coherentism*, is characterized by two theses, viz. (i) that our degree of confidence in the content of a set of propositions is positively affected by the coherence of the set, and (ii) that coherence can be characterized in probabilistic terms. There has been a longstanding question of how to construct a measure of coherence. We will show that Bayesian Coherentism cannot rest on a single measure of coherence, but requires a vector whose components exhaustively characterize the coherence properties of the set. Our degree of confidence in the content of the information set is a function of the reliability of the sources and the components of the coherence vector. The components of this coherence vector are weakly but not strongly separable, which blocks the construction of a single coherence measure.

1. INTRODUCTION

Suppose that we have obtained various items of information from independent sources that are not fully reliable. Let an *information set* be a set containing such items of information. What does it mean to say that our degree of confidence is positively affected by the coherence of the information set? Certainly it need not be the case that coherence is the only determinant of our degree of confidence. For instance, the degree of confidence will also be determined by how reliable we take our information sources to be. Presumably there will be a range of sentences that fit the following schema:

(S) The greater X, the greater our degree of confidence will be that the content of the information set is true, *ceteris paribus*.

The *ceteris paribus* clause assumes that we keep all the other determinants of the degree of confidence of the information set fixed (cf. Bovens and Olsson, 2002). We will investigate what ought to be filled in for X, i.e. what the determinants are of our degree of confidence. It will turn out that one of these determinants is a reliability measure and the other determinants are various components of coherence, expressed in a vector of length n for information sets of size n.

2. NOTATION AND TECHNICAL PRELIMINARIES

(i) Let $S^{(n)}$ be an information set $\{R_1, R_2, \ldots, R_n\}$. We construct propositional variables $R_1, R_2, \ldots, R_n$ whose positive values are the propositions in the information set and whose negative values are their respective negations. In Figure 1, we represent a probability distribution over the propositional variables R_1, R_2, R_3. We introduce the parameters a_i for $i = 0, \ldots, n$: a_i is the probability that $n - i$ of the propositional variables will take on positive values and i propositional variables will take on negative values. Clearly, $\sum_{i=0}^{n} a_i = 1$. We stipulate that the information is neither inconsistent nor certain, i.e. $a_0 \in (0,1)$. Let's call $\langle a_0, \ldots, a_n \rangle$ the *weight vector* of the information set $S^{(n)}$. Let $REPR_i$ be the propositional variable whose positive value is that there is a report to the effect that R_i and whose negative value is that there is no report to the effect that R_i.

(ii) When we are informed that some proposition is true, our source may be more or less reliable. Think of an information source as of a medical test that yields certain proportions for false positives and for false negatives. The reliability of an information source *with*

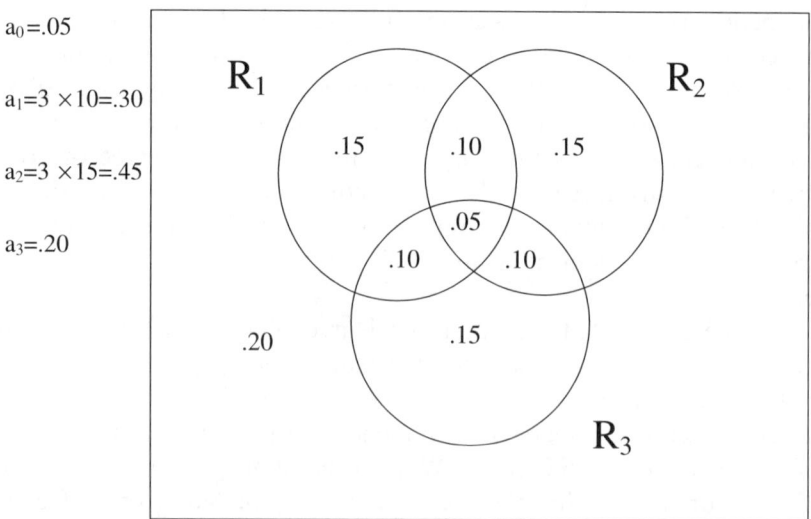

$a_0 = .05$

$a_1 = 3 \times 10 = .30$

$a_2 = 3 \times 15 = .45$

$a_3 = .20$

Figure 1. A diagram of the joint probability distribution over the variables R_1, R_2, and R_3.

respect to the report in question[1] can be readily expressed by the likelihood ratio

(1) $x_i = \dfrac{q_i}{p_i}$ for all sources $i = 1, \ldots, n,$

in which $q_i = P(REPR_i | \neg R_i)$ is the chance of a false positive and $1 - p_i = 1 - P(REPR_i | R_i)$ is the chance of a false negative. For an excellent medical test or information source, $x_i = 0/1 = 0$, whereas for a test or source that is no better than random, $q_i = p_i$ and so $x_i = 1$. Hence we propose $r_i = 1 - x_i$ as a measure of reliability. We exclude fully reliable and fully unreliable information sources: $r \in (0,1)$ and make the idealization that all sources are equally reliable, i.e. $r_i = r$ for all $i = 1, \ldots, n.$[2]

(iii) The coherence of an information set only affects our degree of confidence when the witnesses are at least to some degree independent. To keep things simple, let us assume that the witnesses are independent. Bovens and Olsson (2000) and Earman (2000) provide the following analysis of independence. To say that witnesses are independent is to say that each R_i *screens off* the $REPR_i$ from all R_js and all $REPR_j$s for $i \neq j$, i.e. $REPR_i$ is probabilistically independent of all R_js and all $REPR_j$s given R_i. What this means in ordinary language is that the witnesses are not influenced by the reports of the others witnesses, nor by facts other than the fact that they are reporting on.

3. INFORMATION SINGLETONS

Let us first consider an information singleton. Suppose that we are informed by a less than fully reliable source that R. What determines our degree of confidence that the information is true? This is just an application of Bayes Theorem. For notational convenience, let $\bar{\varphi}$ stand for $1 - \varphi$ for any parameter φ.

(2) $P^*(R) = P(R | REPR) = \dfrac{a_0}{a_0 + \overline{a_0}\,\bar{r}}$

Thereare two determinants to the degree of confidence for singletons, viz. r and a_0. a_0 can be thought of as a measure of external coherence, i.e. a measure of how well the new item of information fits in with our background beliefs. Hence for information singletons, we can fill in the schema in (S):

[71]

(Det$_1$) The greater the *reliability* of the source, i.e. r, the greater our degree of confidence will be that the content of the information set is true, *ceteris paribus*.

(Det$_2$) The greater the *external coherence* of the new item of information with our background beliefs, i.e a_0, the greater our degree of confidence will be that the content of the information set is true, *ceteris paribus*.

The *ceteris paribus* clause in (Det$_1$) requires that we keep a_0 fixed, whereas in (Det$_2$) it requires that we keep r fixed. To show that these claims are true, we calculate the partial derivatives with respect to the respective measures of reliability and the measure of coherence:

$$(3) \qquad \frac{\partial P^*(\mathrm{R})}{\partial r} = \frac{\bar{r}}{a_0^2} P^{*2}(\mathrm{R})$$

$$(4) \qquad \frac{\partial P^*(\mathrm{R})}{\partial a_0} = \frac{\overline{a_0}}{a_0} P^{*2}(\mathrm{R}).$$

Since a_0, r, $P^*(\mathrm{R}) \in (0,1)$, these partial derivatives are both positive, which confirms (Det$_1$) and (Det$_2$).

What seems somewhat trivial at this point, but will become highly relevant for larger information sets, is that (Det$_1$) and (Det$_2$) *both* need to be included in (S). Suppose that we would only include (Det$_1$). Then the *ceteris paribus* claim would be vacuously true, since no other determinants are in play. But (Det$_1$) by itself would be false: Certainly we could imagine that we would be more confident that a new item of information from a less reliable source is true than from a more reliable source, when this item has a much higher degree of external coherence, i.e. it fits in so much better with our background knowledge.

4. INFORMATION PAIRS

Let us now turn to information pairs. Suppose that we are informed by two independent and less than fully reliable sources that R_1 and R_2, respectively. By applying Bayes Theorem and working out the independences, it can be shown[3] that our degree of confidence that both R_1 and R_2 are true after receiving the items of information equals

$$(5) \qquad P^*(R_1, R_2) := P(R_1, R_2 | REPR_1, REPR_2)$$

$$= \frac{a_0}{a_0 + a_1 \bar{r} + a_2 \bar{r}^2} \text{ with } a_2 = 1 - a_0 - a_1$$

There are three determinants to the degree of confidence for pairs, viz. r and a_0 and the degree of *internal coherence* between R_1 and R_2. The internal coherence of $S^{(2)} = \{R_1, R_2\}$ could be measured as follows:

$$(6) \qquad m(S^{(2)}) = \frac{P(R_1, R_2)}{P(R_1 \vee R_2)} = \frac{a_0}{a_0 + a_1}$$

$m(S^{(2)})$ measures the proportional overlap between R_1 and R_2 in the probability space. (This measure is suggested as a possible measure of coherence in Olsson (2002): 250). When we keep a_0 fixed, the measure increases as the marginal probabilities of $P(R_1)$ and $P(R_2)$ decrease, and hence when R_1 and R_2 become the more coherent. When R_1 and R_2 are minimally coherent, i.e. when they are mutually exclusive, then the measure equals 0 and when they are maximally coherent, i.e. when they are equivalent, the measure equals 1.

We can now make a clear statement of the determinants of our degree of confidence for information pairs:

(Det$_1$) The greater the *reliability* of the sources, i.e. r, the greater our degree of confidence will be that the content of the information set is true, *ceteris paribus*.

(Det$_2$) The greater the *external coherence* of the new items of information, i.e a_0, the greater our degree of confidence will be that the content of the information set is true, *ceteris paribus*.

(Det$_3$) The greater the *internal coherence* of the new items of information, i.e $m(S^{(2)})$, the greater our degree of confidence will be that the content of the information set is true, *ceteris paribus*.

These claims are all true: Following the standard procedure, the reader can easily verify that the partial derivatives of $P^*(R_1, R_2)$ with respect to the measures of reliability, external coherence and internal coherence are always positive. (The proof follows from a general proof that will be provided in Section 5.)

Furthermore, any proper subset of conditions {(Det$_1$), (Det$_2$), (Det$_3$)} fails to hold, because it restricts the reach of the *ceteris paribus* clause. The most interesting counterexample is a counterexample to the conditions $\{(\mathrm{Det}_1), (\mathrm{Det}_3)\}$. Since we do not include (Det_2), there is no reason to keep a_0 fixed. Consider the following two information pairs. The information pairs S and S' are characterized by the following vectors $\langle a_0, a_1, a_2 \rangle = \langle .20, .70, .10 \rangle$ and $\langle a'_0, a'_1, a'_2 \rangle = \langle .10, .10, .80 \rangle$. We plot the posterior joint probabilities of S and S' for different values of r in Figure 2. Note that for some values of r, the posterior joint probability of S exceeds the posterior joint probability of S', while for other values of r, the posterior joint probability of S' exceeds the posterior joint probability of S. Hence, it is false to say that the reliability and the internal coherence are *the* relevant determinants of our degree of confidence. The *ceteris paribus* clause does not force us to keep the external coherence fixed, i.e. to set $a_0 = a'_0$. Figure 2 lets us make both a weaker and a stronger objection in response to the claim that the set $\{(\mathrm{Det}_1),$ $(\mathrm{Det}_3)\}$ contains *the* determinants of our degree of confidence. The weaker objection is that it is false to say that the greater the internal coherence, as measured by $m(S)$, the greater our degree of confidence, *ceteris paribus*: $m(S') = 1/2 > 2/9 = m(S)$ and yet, for $r \in (0, 2/3)$, the posterior joint probability of S exceeds the posterior joint probability of S'. The stronger objection is that it is false to say that the greater the internal coherence, *as measured by any probabilistic measure*, the greater our degree of confidence, *ceteris paribus*. A single measure of internal coherence will impose an ordering over S and S', and yet for some values of r, the posterior joint probability of S will exceed the posterior joint probability of S', while for other

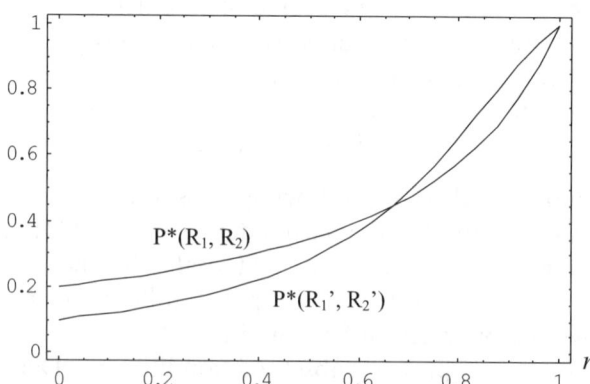

Figure 2. The posterior probability for information pairs with vectors $\langle a_0, a_1, a_2 \rangle = \langle .20, .70, .10 \rangle$ and $\langle a'_0, a'_1, a'_2 \rangle = \langle .10, .10, .80 \rangle$ as a function of the reliability parameter r.

values of r, the posterior joint probability of S will exceed the posterior joint probability of S'.

5. GENERALIZING TO INFORMATION N-TUPLES

One might be tempted to think that we have now found the determinants of our degrees of confidence, viz. reliability, external and internal coherence. The measure $m(S^{(2)})$ in (6) can be readily generalized to $m(S^{(n)})$:

$$(7) \qquad m(S^{(n)}) = \frac{P(R_1, \ldots, R_n)}{P(R_1 \vee \ldots \vee R_n)} = \frac{a_0}{\sum_{i=0}^{n-1} a_i} = \frac{a_0}{1 - a_n}$$

Furthermore, it is easy to show[4] that the formula in (5) generalizes to

$$(8) \qquad P(R_1, \ldots, R_n | REPR_1, \ldots, REPR_n) = \frac{a_0}{\sum_{i=0}^{n} a_i \bar{r}^i}.$$

We can now rephrase (Det$_3$):

(Det$_3'$) The greater the *internal coherence* of the new items of information, i.e $m(S^{(n)})$, the greater our degree of confidence will be that the content of the information set is true, *ceteris paribus*.

{(Det$_1$), (Det$_2$), (Det$_3'$)} is then the set of *all* determinants of our degree of confidence.

This turns out to be a mistake. To see that this is a mistake, let us assume for a second that this were true for information triples. To show that {(Det$_1$), (Det$_2$), (Det$_3'$)} does not hold for information triples, pick any two triples S and S' with probability distributions so that $\langle a_0, a_1, a_2, a_3 \rangle = \langle .05, .3, .1, .55 \rangle$ and $\langle a_0', a_1', a_2', a_3' \rangle = \langle .05, .2, .7, .05 \rangle$. Notice that the external coherence of both information sets is held fixed, i.e. $a_0 = a_0'$. We plot the posterior probability of these two information sets for different values of r in Figure 3. Again, we can make a weaker objection and a stronger objection. The weaker objection is that it is false to say that the greater the internal coherence, as measured by $m(S)$, the greater our degree of confidence, *ceteris paribus*: $m(S) = .05/.45 > .05/.95 = m(S')$ and yet, for $r \in (.8, 1)$, the posterior joint probability of S' exceeds the posterior joint probability of S. The stronger objection is that it is false to say

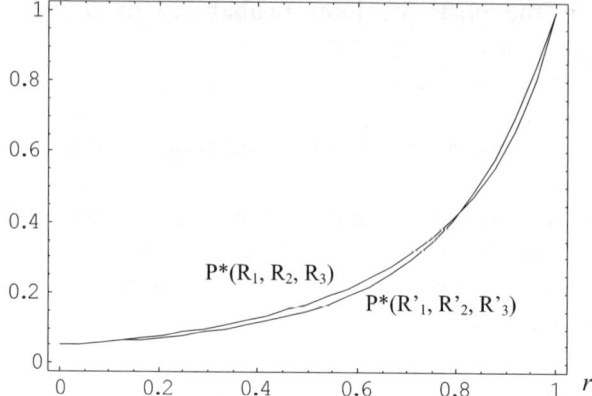

Figure 3. The posterior probability for information triples with weight vectors $\langle a_0, a_1, a_2, a_3 \rangle = \langle .05, .3, .1, .55 \rangle$ and $\langle a_0', a_1', a_2', a_3' \rangle = \langle .05, .2, .7, .05 \rangle$ as a function of the reliability parameter r.

that the greater the internal coherence, *as measured by any probabilistic measure*, the greater our degree of confidence, *ceteris paribus*. A measure of internal coherence will impose an ordering over S and S′, and yet for some values of r, the posterior joint probability of S will exceed the posterior joint probability of S′, while for other values of r, the posterior joint probability of S will exceed the posterior joint probability of S′.

So what can be done for information triples? Note that for information singletons, there is a unary vector of coherence determinants of the posterior probability, viz. $\langle a_0 \rangle$; for information pairs there is a binary vector of coherence determinants, viz. $\langle a_0/(a_0 + a_1), a_0 \rangle$. We can make the following generalization. The vector of coherence determinants for information n-tuples contains the following n components: the ratio of the joint probability a_0 over the probability that *at least* i of the n propositions are true for $i = n - 1$, this same ratio for $i = n - 2, \ldots$, this same ratio for $i = 0$. For singletons, this is the vector $\langle a_0 \rangle$. For pairs this is the vector $\langle a_0/(a_0 + a_1), a_0 \rangle$. For triples, this is the vector $\langle a_0/(a_0 + a_1), a_0/(a_0 + a_1 + a_2), a_0 \rangle$. For n-tuples, this is the vector $\langle a_0/(a_0 + a_1), \ldots, a_0/(a_0 + a_1 + \cdots + a_{n-1}), a_0 \rangle$. This can be represented by means of the following shorthand. Let

$$(9) \qquad c_k = \frac{a_0}{\displaystyle\sum_{i=0}^{k} a_i} \quad \text{for } k = 1, \ldots, n.$$

We can define a vector that contains the internal coherence determinants,

$$(10) \quad \vec{c}^{\,\text{int}} = \langle c_1, \ldots, c_{n-1} \rangle,$$

and an encompassing vector that contains both the internal coherence determinants and the external coherence determinant $c^{\text{ext}} = c_n = a_0$:

$$(11) \quad \vec{c} = \langle c_1, \ldots, c_n \rangle = \langle \vec{c}^{\,\text{int}}, c^{\text{ext}} \rangle$$

Does this generalization for n-tuples hold? We will follow the standard procedure and show that the partial derivatives of $P^*(R_1, \ldots, R_n)$ with respect to r, and all c_ks (for $k = 1, \ldots, n$) are all positive. First we present a representation of $P^*(R_1, \ldots, R_n)$ in (12) that is more convenient to calculate the partial derivatives (proof omitted):

$$(12) \quad P^*(R_1, \ldots, R_n) = \cfrac{1}{r \sum\limits_{i=0}^{n-1} \dfrac{\vec{r}^{\,i}}{c_i} + \dfrac{\vec{r}^{\,n}}{c_n}}$$

We calculate the partial derivatives:

$$(13) \quad \frac{\partial P^*(R_1, \ldots, R_n)}{\partial r} = \sum_{i=1}^{n} i \left(\frac{1}{c_i} - \frac{1}{c_{i-1}} \right) \vec{r}^{\,i-1} P^{*2}(R_1, \ldots, R_n)$$

$$(14) \quad \frac{\partial P^*(R_1, \ldots, R_n)}{\partial c_n} = \frac{\vec{r}^{\,n}}{c_n^2} P^{*2}(R_1, \ldots, R_n)$$

$$(15) \quad \frac{\partial P^*(R_1, \ldots, R_n)}{\partial c_k} = \frac{r \vec{r}^{\,k}}{c_k^2} P^{*2}(R_1, \ldots, R_n) \text{ for } k = 1, \ldots, n-1$$

Since $r, P^*(R_1, \ldots, R_n) \in (0, 1)$ and $c_i < c_{i-1}$ for $i = 1, \ldots, n$, these expressions are all greater than 0. This confirms that the following are the determinants for our degree of confidence that the content of an information n-tuple is true are (Det$_1$), (Det$_2$) and for all $i = 1, \ldots, n-1$,

(Det$_{2+i}$) The greater the component of the internal coherence of the new items of information that is measured by c_i, the greater our degree of confidence will be that the content of the information set is true, *ceteris paribus*.

Note that $c_k = P(R_1, \ldots, R_n |$ at least $n - k$ propositions true). Note further that an expression similar to eq. (15) holds if c_k is replaced by $t_k = c_k / a_0$. t_k is the ratio measure which is a common way to measure how well the information set $\{R_1, \ldots, R_n\}$ is supported by the evidence that at least $n - k$ propositions are true. Dietrich and Moretti (forthcoming) have already pointed out that there is an interesting relation between coherence and confirmation. We plan to elaborate on this in future work in the context of our criterion for a coherence quasi-ordering (Bovens and Hartmann: 2003a, b).

6. SEPARABILITY

So where did things go wrong in the attempt to measure coherence? There seems to be a focus on finding a single measure of coherence. This is a mistake. First, we need to have both external and internal measures of coherence, already when the information sets that are being compared are just pairs. One might argue that an external coherence measure is really not a coherence measure but rather a measure of how *plausible* or *expected* the new information is.[5] But this is just a verbal dispute and it is certainly not entirely implausible to say that a_0 is a coherence measure, because it measures how well the new information coheres with our background beliefs. What is important is that we can characterize a_0, which we have dubbed "a measure of external coherence", as the last entry in a vector of measures that are governed by a common mathematical structure. Second, as the information set grows, we need multiple complementary internal measures of coherence. The posterior probability of the information set of size n is determined by a reliability measure and a vector of n coherence determinants.

Borrowing from preference theory, there is a very concise way of spelling out the point that we have made in this paper, viz. the probabilistic determinants of our degrees of confidence are *weakly*, but not *strongly separable*.[6] What does this mean? Let us construct a simple illustration in preference theory. Suppose that I have two baskets with wine, vodka and cheese. When my preferences are weakly separable, then the following holds:

(Weak Separability) Take any two pairs of baskets $\{B_1, B_2\}$ and $\{B'_1,$
    $B'_2\}$. For all commodities i, the following holds true. Let B_1 and B'_1

contain the same amount of a particular commodity i and similarly for B_2 and B_2'. Furthermore, let B_1 and B_2 contain the same amounts of all other commodities $j \neq i$ and similarly for B_1' and B_2'. Then $B_1 \succ B_2$ iff $B_1' \succ B_2'$.

When my preferences are strongly separable, then the following holds true:

(Strong Separability) Take any two pairs of baskets $\{B_1, B_2\}$ and $\{B_1', B_2'\}$. Let C be the set of types of commodities. For all proper subsets of types of commodities $c \subset C$, the following holds true. Let B_1 and B_1' contain the same amounts of all types of commodities in a particular c and similarly for B_2 and B_2'. Furthermore, let B_1 and B_2 contain the same amounts of all types of commodities in the complement of c and similarly for B_1' and B_2'. Then $B_1 \succ B_2$ iff $B_1' \succ B_2'$.

How is it that my preferences over commodities could be weakly but not strongly separable? To be weakly separable it is sufficient that if one basket contains more of some commodity than another basket, *ceteris paribus* (i.e. keeping the amounts of all other commodities fixed), then I prefer the former to the latter. If there is no distinction between the amounts of any of the other items, then a basket with more wine is better than a basket with less wine. And similarly for vodka and for cheese. But strong separability imposes a stronger requirement. Let c be the commodities wine and vodka. Let B_1 and B_1' contain the same amounts of wine and vodka, viz. lots of wine and little vodka, and let B_2 and B_2' contain the same amounts of wine and vodka, viz. lots of vodka and little wine. Furthermore, let B_1 and B_2 contain the same amounts of cheese, viz. lots and let B_1' and B_2' contain the same amounts of cheese, viz. little. Considering that wine and cheese mix better than wine and vodka, one might expect that $B_1 \succ B_2$ and $B_2' \succ B_1'$. This is a violation of strong separability.

When our preferences are weakly separable, we can construct utility functions u_i over each commodity so that our preferences over baskets can be expressed by a function U of the utility functions over each commodity. In addition, Debreu (1960) (as cited in Broome, 1991: 70) has shown that there exist functions u_i so that U is an additive function if and only if our preferences are also strongly separable. So if our preferences are strongly separable, then we could construct a preference ordering over the baskets *only with respect to their liquid content – i.e. their content of wine and vodka*. We could simply take the sum of the additive utility values for wine and vodka to reflect such an ordering. But this is not possible when our preferences are only weakly separable: There will be some pairs of baskets which we cannot order with respect to their liquid content, since the direction of the ordering is contingent on the amount of cheese.

Let us now turn back to the probabilistic determinants of our degrees of confidence. Certainly these determinants are weakly separable: The partial derivatives show that if one information set scores higher on some determinant than another information set, *ceteris paribus* – i.e. keeping all the other determinants fixed – then the posterior probability of the former will be higher than of the latter. What our counter examples show is that strong separability between these measures does not hold. To see this, consider the pairs of information sets S and S' with their associated weight vectors $\langle a_0, \ldots, a_n \rangle$ and $\langle a_0', \ldots, a_n' \rangle$ in our counter examples. It was not possible to order these vectors so that $P^*(R_1, \ldots, R_n)$ is greater than $P^*(R_1', \ldots, R_n')$ (or vice versa) for *all* values of r. Hence, it is impossible to order the coherence vectors $\langle a_0/(a_0+a_1), \ldots, a_0/(a_0+a_1 + \cdots + a_{n-1}), a_0 \rangle$ and   so that $P^*(R_1, \ldots, R_n)$ is greater than $P^*(R_1', \ldots R_n')$ (or vice versa) for all values of r. This is a violation of strong separability.

Let us return to our example from economics now to see what the lack of strong separability means for our assessment of coherence. If my preferences over commodities are not strongly separable, then there are certain pairs of baskets that I cannot order according to their liquid content, *ceteris paribus* – i.e. under the assumption that their cheese contents are held fixed: It depends on the amount of cheese in these baskets whether I will prefer one basket over the other. We have shown that the determinants of my degree of confidence in the content of an information set are not strongly separable. If coherence is the property of an information set that increases my degree of confidence in the content of the information set, *ceteris paribus*, then the following holds. There are certain pairs of information sets that I cannot order according to their coherence. Some pairs are such that my degree of confidence in one information set will be greater for some degrees of reliability, while my degree of confidence in the other information set will be greater for other degrees of reliability.

On the other hand, there *are* certain pairs of baskets which I *can* order according to their liquid content: I don't need to see how much cheese there is to know that I prefer the basket with lots of wine and vodka to the basket with little wine and vodka, as long as both baskets contain the same amounts of cheese. Similarly, there are certain pairs of information sets S and S' that I can order according to which one is more coherent: I don't need to know how reliable the informers are to know that my degree of confidence in the content of S will exceed my degree of confidence in the content of S', as long as they are equally reliable. Hence, just like we can construct a quasi-ordering over the baskets according to their liquid content, we can construct a quasi-ordering over the information sets according to their coherence. Under what conditions we can and cannot impose an ordering on a pair of information sets is an interesting question, but beyond the scope of this paper.[7,8]

NOTES

[1] This is different from the reliability of an information source *tout court*. To see this distinction consider the case in which $q = 0$. In this case, r will reach its maximal value, no matter what the value of p is. Certainly a source that provides fewer rather than more false negatives, as measured by $1 - p$, is a more reliable source *tout court*. But when q is 0, the reliability *with respect to the report in question* is not affected by the value of $p > 0$. No matter what the value of p is, we can be fully confident that what the source says is true, since $q = 0$ – i.e. the source never provides any false positives. When we speak of the reliability of the sources, we will mean the reliability of the source *with respect to the report in question*, rather than the reliability of the source *tout court*.

[2] For a justification of the assumption of equal reliability in determining a measure of coherence, see Bovens and Hartmann (2003b: 45–47).

[3] The proof is straightforward: Apply Bayes Theorem; simplify on grounds of the independences in the screening off condition and substitute in the parameters p and q; divide numerator and denominator by p^2; substitute in the parameters r and a_i for $i = 0$, 1, and 2.

[4] See Bovens and Hartmann (2003a: 607–10 and 2003b: 131–133).

[5] See Bovens and Hartmann (2003a: 605 and b: 10).

[6] For an introduction to separability, see Broome (1991: 60–89).

[7] Note that our procedure is different than in Bovens and Hartmann (2003a, b) and that it will not yield the same coherence quasi-ordering. The reason is that we conceive of coherence here as covering both external and internal coherence, whereas, in Bovens and Hartmann (2003a: 605–606 and b: 10–11), we distinguish between the *expectedness* of the information – which corresponds to the external coherence – and the *coherence* – which corresponds to the internal coherence. The term *coherence* is ambiguous in ordinary language. Suppose that one is told that AIDS is caused by malnutrition and that AIDS is due to a vitamin-B deficiency. Is this information coherent? Well, yes and no. Yes, because one might say that, though the information is implausible, given my background knowledge about AIDS, this does not stand in the way of proclaiming that the information is coherent. This is the notion of coherence that is analyzed in (2003a, 2003b). No, because one might say that this information coheres very poorly with one's background knowledge.

Granted, the information items cohere well between themselves, but this internal coherence is not sufficient to make us proclaim that the information is coherent. This is the notion that is analyzed in this paper.

[8] We are grateful for the support of the Alexander von Humboldt Foundation, the Federal Ministry of Education and Research and the Program for the Investment in the Future (ZIP) of the German Government through a Sofja Kovalevskaja Award.

REFERENCES

Bovens, L. and S. Hartmann: 2003a, 'Solving the Riddle of Coherence', *Mind* **112**, 601–634.

Bovens, L. and S. Hartmann: 2003b, *Bayesian Epistemology*, Oxford University Press, Oxford.

Bovens, L. and E. J. Olsson: 2000, 'Coherentism, Reliability and Bayesian Networks', *Mind* **109**, 685–719.

Bovens, L. and E. J. Olsson: 2002, 'Believing More, Risking Less – On Coherence, Truth and Non-Trivial Extensions', *Erkenntnis* **52**, 137–150.

Broome, J.: 1991, *Weighing Goods*, Blackwell, Oxford.

Debreu, G.: 1960, 'Topological Methods in Cardinal Utility Theory', in Kenneth J. Arrow, Samuel Karlin and Patrick Suppes (eds.): 1959, *Mathematical Methods in the Social Sciences 1959: Proceedings of the First Stanford Symposium*. Stanford University Press, Stanford, pp. 16–26.

Earman, J.: 2000, *Hume's Abject Failure*, Oxford University Press, Oxford.

Dietrich, F. and L. Moretti: 2006, 'On Coherent Sets and the Transmission of Confirmation', *Philosophy of Science* **72**(3), 403–424.

Olsson, E. J.: 2001, 'Why Coherence is not Truth-Conducive', *Analysis* **61**, 186–193.

Olsson, E. J.: 2002, 'What is the Problem of Coherence and Truth?', *Journal of Philosophy* **94**, 246–272.

Department of Philosophy,
Logic, and Scientific Method
London School of Economics and Political Science
Houghton Street
London, WC2A 2AE, UK
E-mail: L.Bovens@LSE.ac.uk
E-mail: S.Hartmann@LSE.ac.uk

Erkenntnis (2005) 63:375–385
DOI 10.1007/s10670-005-4000-6

DAVID H. GLASS

PROBLEMS WITH PRIORS IN PROBABILISTIC MEASURES OF COHERENCE

ABSTRACT. Two of the probabilistic measures of coherence discussed in this paper take probabilistic dependence into account and so depend on prior probabilities in a fundamental way. An example is given which suggests that this prior-dependence can lead to potential problems. Another coherence measure is shown to be independent of prior probabilities in a clearly defined sense and consequently is able to avoid such problems. The issue of prior-dependence is linked to the fact that the first two measures can be understood as measures of coherence as *striking* agreement, while the third measure represents coherence as agreement. Thus, prior (in)dependence can be used to distinguish different conceptions of coherence.

1. INTRODUCTION

It has proved remarkably difficult to provide a satisfactory definition of coherence even though there is agreement about some of the features such a definition should possess. Since the coherence of a set of beliefs is a matter of degree and involves the relationship between those beliefs, it is tempting to think that a probabilistic account can be given. In recent papers Shogenji (1999), Olsson (2002) and Fitelson (2003) have adopted this strategy and proposed probabilistic measures of coherence, while Akiba (2000), Bovens and Hartmann (2003, Section 2.6)[1] and Siebel (2004) have presented a number of criticisms. An important criterion for any adequate measure of coherence is that it should provide a satisfactory account of the coherence of n beliefs in the general case where $n \geq 2$. However, in this paper the discussion is limited to the case of two beliefs. There are two main reasons for this rather severe restriction. First, there is no agreement concerning coherence measures even in this case. Second, there are two distinct ways of characterising coherence for more than two beliefs: one approach takes into account only the n-way coherence (Shogenji, 1999), while the other approach considers the j-way coherence for all $j \leq n$ (Fitelson, 2003). By focussing on the simpler problem of two beliefs, I hope to clarify some issues that might also be relevant in the general case.

In this paper I concentrate mainly on Fitelson's measure and argue that potential problems arise as a result of the way in which it depends on prior probabilities. I then consider an alternative coherence measure that overcomes these problems since it is independent (in a well-defined sense) of prior probabilities. Further analysis shows that this notion of independence can be used to distinguish two fundamentally different conceptions of coherence.

2. FITELSON'S COHERENCE MEASURE

Intuitively the coherence of two beliefs A and B tells us something about how well they fit together or give support to each other. Taking this idea into account, Fitelson bases his measure of coherence on a modification of Kemeny and Oppenheim's (1952) measure of factual support F. The degree to which B supports A can be written as

$$
(1) \quad F(A,B) = \begin{cases} \dfrac{P(B|A)-P(B|{\sim}A)}{P(B|A)+P(B|{\sim}A)}, & \text{if A is contingent and} \\ & \text{B is not a necessary falsehood} \\ 1, & \text{if A and B are necessary truths} \\ 0, & \text{if A is a necessary truth and} \\ & \text{B is contingent} \\ -1, & \text{if B is a necessary falsehood} \end{cases}
$$

This expression can then be used to define the coherence measure, C_1, for a set of beliefs, which in the case of two beliefs A and B is

$$
(2) \quad C_1(A,B) = \frac{1}{2}\{F(A,B) + F(B,A)\}.
$$

Fitelson intends his measure to be a probabilistic generalisation of logical coherence and as such it should respect the extreme deductive cases. Note that values of C_1 lie in the interval $[-1,1]$ with the value of 1 obtained if A and B are logically equivalent and satisfiable and -1 if they are logically inconsistent. Thus, in addition to capturing the idea of mutual support, Fitelson's measure treats these extreme cases in an appropriate manner.

A further claim made by Fitelson is that a probabilistic generalisation of logical coherence should be "properly sensitive to probabilistic dependence". To meet this requirement he develops an account of independence which, unlike the standard account, is able to deal with non-contingent beliefs. Two beliefs A and B are independent if and only if $F(A,B) = 0$ and $F(B,A) = 0$. Furthermore, they are positively(negatively) dependent if and only if F(A,B) and F(B,A) are both positive(negative). In the case of independence $C_1(A,B)=0$, while in the case of positive(negative) dependence $C_1(A,B)$ is positive(negative). Thus, there is a close connection between the value of coherence as given by C_1 and the dependence relationship among the beliefs under consideration.[2]

All of the features mentioned so far make C_1 a very plausible candidate as a measure of coherence. The features of mutual support and the proper treatment of the deductive cases seem to be reasonable requirements for a coherence measure, especially if coherence is to be understood as a probabilistic generalisation of logical coherence. It also seems perfectly reasonable to expect that such a measure should include the notion of probabilistic (in)dependence. However, while the notion of probabilistic (in)dependence is central to Fitelson's account, it does give rise to potential problems as discussed below.

3. PROBLEMS WITH PRIOR DEPENDENCE

Coherence seems to be concerned with the extent to which beliefs agree with each other. By contrast, it is far from clear whether it should depend on how probable those beliefs are in the first place. This raises a question concerning the role prior probabilities should play in coherence measures. It is important to note that dependence on priors is not an all-or-nothing affair, but can occur in different ways and to different extents. Consider Shogenji's coherence measure, for example, which for two beliefs is given by,

$$(3) \qquad C_2(A,B) = \frac{P(A \wedge B)}{P(A)P(B)}.$$

Fitelson points out an inappropriate dependence on the prior probability in the C_2-measure in the case where the beliefs are logically equivalent. Consider logical equivalence for two beliefs where $P(A)=P(B)=p$. In this case the C_2-measure yields the value $1/p$. Fitelson's C_1-measure yields the maximal value of 1 in this case, which seems correct since logically equivalent beliefs are in complete agreement with each other and so it might be expected that they would be maximally coherent.

Akiba considers the case where A entails B. The C_2-measure yields the value $1/P(B)$, which Fitelson notes is "unintuitive, since it only depends on the unconditional probability of [B]." The problem here is that the C_2-measure depends only on the prior probability of B rather than on the relation between the beliefs. By contrast the C_1-measure yields the value $1/(1 + P(B|{\sim}A))$ and so overcomes the problem. This is an improvement on Shogenji's result in this case, and as in the case of logical equivalence, indicates problems that can arise for Shogenji's measure due to the nature of its dependence on prior probabilities.

While Fitelson's C_1-measure does not depend on priors in the same way as Shogenji's measure, that is not to say that it does not depend on priors at all. This raises the question as to whether the remaining prior dependence in the C_1-measure is innocuous. The following example illustrates a potential problem with the C_1-measure, which suggests that it too might suffer from an inappropriate dependence on priors. Consider the example from Akiba's paper, where a die is rolled and the beliefs A and B are,

> A: it will come up 2,
>
> B: it will come up 2 or 4.

According to the C_1-measure the coherence is $1/(1 + (1/5)) = 5/6$. Note that in this case $P(B|A) = 1$, $P(A|B) = 1/2$, $P(A) = 1/6$ and $P(B) = 1/3$. Now consider the same beliefs, but instead a dodecahedron is rolled. In this case, the C_1-measure yields the result $1/(1 + 1/11) = 11/12$ and so the coherence is greater than in the case of the die.[3] But what has changed? Crucially, the prior probabilities have changed ($P(A) = 1/12$ and $P(B) = 1/6$), while the conditional probabilities remain the same ($P(B|A) = 1$ and $P(A|B) = 1/2$). This example suggests that there might be an inappropriate dependence on prior probabilities in Fitelson's account (as there is in Shogenji's[4]). Furthermore, this dependence could not be removed within Fitelson's framework since it relies on the notion of factual support which, as defined, requires the value for $P(B|{\sim}A)$ when considering the factual support for A provided by B. It is this probability (and $P(A|{\sim}B)$) that gives rise to the dependence on the prior probability of A (and B).

One line of response open to Fitelson, as well as Shogenji, in light of this alleged problem, depends on the distinction between coherence as agreement and coherence as *striking* agreement (Bovens and Olsson, 2000). Coherence as striking agreement refers to a conception of coherence that is sensitive to the specificity of the information, while this is not the case for coherence as agreement. As an example, Bovens and Olsson (2000) consider a roulette wheel with one hundred numbers. In the first scenario, Joe says the winning number is 49 or

50 and Amy says it is 50 or 51. In the second, scenario Joe says the winning number is 1, 2, ..., or 70 and Amy says it is 31, 32, ..., or 100. Are the claims of Joe and Amy more coherent in scenario one or scenario two? If coherence is taken to be coherence as agreement, their claims are more coherent in scenario two since the degree of overlap is greater. However, if coherence is taken to be coherence as striking agreement, their claims are more coherent in scenario one since the claims in scenario one are much more specific (even though the degree of overlap is slightly smaller).

Perhaps the C_1 and C_2-measures are intended to be measures of coherence as striking agreement, whereas the criticism offered in the example given above presupposes a view of coherence as agreement.[5] Furthermore, even if Fitelson and Shogenji both give measures of coherence as striking agreement, there are also further differences in the conceptions of coherence that they have in mind. The purpose in the rest of this paper is to focus on a measure of coherence as agreement and to explore some important differences between it and the measures discussed so far.

4. A PRIOR INDEPENDENT COHERENCE MEASURE

The discussion in Section 3 suggests that a measure of coherence as agreement should be independent of prior probabilities. This, however, seems like an impossible requirement since the only alternative for a probabilistic measure of coherence is that it should depend on conditional probabilities, but these of course depend on priors as Bayes' theorem makes clear. Nevertheless, there is a precise sense in which a coherence measure can be prior independent: if, for two probability distributions P and P' on A and B, $P(A|B)=P'(A|B)$ and $P(B|A)=P'(B|A)$, then a coherence measure should assign the pair {A,B} the same coherence relative to P and P'.[6] A simple definition of coherence, C_3, that satisfies this requirement has been discussed by Olsson (2002) and Glass (2002) and for two beliefs is given by

$$(4) \quad C_3(A,B) = \frac{P(A \wedge B)}{P(A \vee B)}$$

provided $P(A \vee B) \neq 0$.[7] Informally, it is the "degree of overlap" that determines the coherence of the beliefs.[8] $C_3(A,B)=0$ when the probability of the conjunction is zero (i.e. there is no overlap). Whenever A entails B and vice-versa, $C_3(A,B)=1$. Thus, C_3 yields a measure on the interval $[0,1]$ with the value of 0 for logically inconsistent beliefs and the value of 1 for beliefs that are logically equivalent and satisfiable.

By using Bayes' theorem and assuming that $P(A \wedge B) \neq 0$, Equation (4) can be rewritten as,

$$(5) \quad \begin{aligned} C_3(A,B) &= \frac{P(A|B)P(B)}{P(A) + P(B) - P(A|B)P(B)} \\ &= \left[\frac{1}{P(A|B)} + \frac{1}{P(B|A)} - 1 \right]^{-1} \end{aligned}$$

Thus the expression for coherence can be expressed in terms of conditional probabilities and so the relationship between the beliefs comes across clearly since coherence increases with increase in the conditional probabilities. Note also that no appeal to prior probabilities is required and so the coherence of A and B does not tell us anything about how likely it is that A and B are true in the first place.

Consider again the die/dodecahedron example discussed in Section 3. C_3 should be able to deal with this case since it was the prior dependence in the coherence measures C_1 and C_2 that caused the problem. Note that $C_3(A,B) = P(A|B)$ in cases where A entails B and so yields a value of $1/2$ in the case of the dodecahedron as well as in the case of the die. The reason for the agreement in the two scenarios is that coherence as given by C_3 only depends on the conditional probabilities.

This crucial distinction between C_1 and C_2, on the one hand, and C_3 on the other in terms of prior dependence/independence is closely related to another fundamental difference between these measures. In their accounts Fitelson and Shogenji stress that there is a neutral point where the pair of beliefs (and also in the general case of n beliefs) are neither coherent nor incoherent and this neutral point is identified as the point of probabilistic independence. Shogenji notes that A and B are probabilistically independent if $P(A|B)/P(A) = 1$ and as a consequence the neutral value of coherence is 1. Fitelson's characterisation of independence differs for non-contingent statements since it requires that $P(A|B) - P(A|\sim B) = 0$ and so the neutral value is 0. Since the neutral points depend on probabilistic independence, the fact that Fitelson's measure has negative values while Shogenji's does not is merely conventional. By contrast, the fact that the C_3-measure of coherence is always positive is highly significant for it has no neutral point.

There seems to be a good reason for bringing probabilistic independence into the picture since it provides a neutral point between logical equivalence and logical contradiction. However, while this might be appropriate for measures of coherence as striking agreement it is problematic for coherence as agreement since it gives rise to the problems associated with the die/dodecahedron example. The reason for this is that there does not seem to be any way of characterising independence that does not depend on prior probabilities in a fundamental way. By contrast, the C_3-measure does not include the prior probabilities and so does not contain any information about the probabilistic dependence of the beliefs. Consequently, it is able to avoid the problem raised by the example. Thus, it seems that the presence or absence of prior-dependence and probabilistic (in)dependence might provide ways of characterising the difference between these two conceptions of coherence.

5. THE BOVENS–OLSSON CONDITION

Bovens and Olsson (2000) set out what they describe as a minimal sufficient condition for the relation "more coherent than" for a set of beliefs {A,B}. Considering two probability distributions P and P' on A and B satisfying the condition that $P(A|B) > P'(A|B)$ and $P(B|A) > P'(B|A)$, they claim that {A,B} is more coherent on distribution P than on distribution P'. Clearly, the Bovens–Olsson condition and the notion of prior independence, as defined in Section 4, are closely related. In fact, prior independence can be understood as a natural extension of the Bovens–Olsson condition to the case where the relevant conditional probabilities are equal. It can be seen from expression (5) that increasing both the conditional probabilities necessarily increases coherence according to the C_3-measure so that $C_3(A,B) > C_3'(A,B)$ i.e. that {A,B} is more C_3-coherent on probability distribution P than on probability distribution P'. Thus, in addition to being prior independent, the C_3-measure satisfies the Bovens–Olsson condition. By using their condition Bovens and Olsson are able to establish a partial ordering of information pairs, whereas the C_3-measure provides a total ordering.

Given that the C_1 and C_2-measures are prior dependent, it might be expected that they would fail to satisfy the Bovens–Olsson condition and this is indeed the case as the following counterexample shows. Consider a die being rolled and the beliefs:

A: the die will come up 1 or 2,

B: the die will come up 2 or 3.

Let P' be the distribution for an unbiased die. For this distribution we find that $P'(A|B) = 1/2$ and $P'(B|A) = 1/2$ and that the coherence measures yield the values $C_1'(A,B) = 1/3$, $C_2'(A,B) = 3/2$ and $C_3'(A,B) = 1/3$. Let P be the distribution for a biased die such that $P(1) = 1/5$, $P(2) = 2/5$, $P(3) = 1/5$, $P(4) = P(5) = P(6) = 1/15$ and so $P(A|B) = 2/3$ and $P(B|A) = 2/3$. For this distribution we find that $C_1(A,B) = 1/7$, $C_2(A,B) = 10/9$ and $C_3(A,B) = 1/2$. Although the conditional probabilities are higher for distribution P than they are for distribution P', C_1 and C_2 are lower for distribution P. Thus, C_1 and C_2 fail to satisfy the Bovens–Olsson condition.

Bovens and Olsson note that one response to their condition is that it applies to coherence as agreement, but not to coherence as striking agreement. This is consistent with our earlier discussion and brings out the connection between three features of coherence measures. The coherence measures C_1 and C_2 depend on prior probabilities, incorporate the idea of probabilistic (in)dependence and fail to satisfy the Bovens–Olsson condition. By contrast C_3 is independent of prior probabilities, does not incorporate any notion of probabilistic (in)dependence and does satisfy the Bovens–Olsson condition. These three features are further linked with the fact that C_3 is a measure of coherence as agreement whereas C_1 and C_2 are perhaps better considered as measures of coherence as striking agreement.

6. THE PROBLEM OF CONJUNCTION

A final point needs to be taken into account since it is a more general criticism of coherence measures. Akiba (2000) points out a very serious concern regarding the C_2-measure, but it applies equally to the C_1 and C_3-measures. To quote Akiba,

... for any two things [A] and [B] we believe, we can also believe one thing, their conjunction, [A ∧ B]. Obviously the coherence of two beliefs [A] and [B] should be no different from the coherence of one conjunctive belief [A ∧ B]; that is, [C(A,B) = C(A ∧ B)]. (Akiba, 2000, p. 358)

If correct, it is a "devastating problem" since none of the coherence measures being considered satisfies Akiba's condition. Here I attempt to show that Akiba's argument is incorrect.[9]

Consider again the example of the die discussed in Section 5. Coherence, C(A,B), describes the relationship between two beliefs.

Crucially, it must take into account not only the extent of agreement between A and B, but also the extent of disagreement between them. For example, in the C_3-measure $P(A \wedge B)$ represents the agreement between A and B, while $P(A \vee B)$ also takes into account disagreement if $P(A \vee B) \neq P(A \wedge B)$. By contrast the coherence of the conjunction describes the coherence of a single belief and it is not even obvious that this makes sense since coherence is primarily a relationship between two beliefs. However, perhaps it does make sense to talk about the coherence of a belief with itself in which case Akiba's claim amounts to saying that $C(A,B) = C(A \wedge B, A \wedge B)$, but this does not seem plausible at all. To see this note that in the die/dodecahedron example in Section 2 the conjunctive belief in question is

$A \wedge B$: the die will come up 2.

Since this belief is in complete agreement with itself, we might expect that $C(A \wedge B, A \wedge B)$ should be maximal. There is no good reason to expect it to be the same as $C(A,B)$, which takes into account disagreement between the beliefs A and B, and so Akiba's argument fails.

7. CONCLUSIONS

In this paper I have considered a number of similarities and some important differences between Fitelson's measure of coherence, C_1, and the C_3-measure discussed in Section 4. Both measures are symmetric, treat the extreme deductive cases appropriately and capture the intuitive idea that coherent beliefs fit together well. However, C_1 takes probabilistic (in)dependence into account and as a result is dependent on prior probabilities. This leads to the problem associated with the example in Section 3 and the fact that C_1 fails to satisfy the Bovens–Olsson condition. By avoiding probabilistic (in)dependence, and hence prior dependence, C_3 is able to avoid these problems. This is important for C_3 since it is intended as a measure of coherence as agreement, whereas C_1 is arguably understood better as a measure of coherence as striking agreement.[10]

ACKNOWLEDGEMENTS

I would like to thank Branden Fitelson, Erik Olsson, Tomoji Shogenji and Alan Weir for extremely helpful comments on earlier drafts of this paper. I am also very grateful to the referees for important suggestions on a number of points.

NOTES

[1] Bovens and Hartmann (2003) give a detailed discussion of the concept of coherence and present their own probabilistic account, which differs in a number of respects from the approaches considered in this paper.

[2] The nature of this link is not quite as clear as it might appear from the discussion above. It turns out that in the case of two beliefs $C_1(A,B) = 0$ if and only if A and B are independent and $C_1(A,B)$ is positive/negative if and only if A and B are positively/negatively dependent. In the case of more than two beliefs, however, these are necessary but not sufficient conditions for the dependence relationship between the beliefs. C_1 could be greater than 0, for example, and yet the beliefs not be positively dependent. It also turns out to be the case that $C_1(A,B) = 1$ if and only if A and B are logically equivalent and satisfiable and $C_1(A,B) = -1$ if and only if A and B are logically inconsistent. Furthermore, it seems to be the case that these conditions for maximal and minimal values also hold for more than two beliefs.

[3] Fitelson (unpublished) has modified his original definition of coherence, but this change has no effect on the values of coherence in this example.

[4] Shogenji's measure, C_2, yields the value 3 in the case of the die and 6 in the case of the dodecahedron and so the C_2-measure has a much stronger prior dependence than the C_1-measure in this case.

[5] Olsson (2002) also draws attention to this distinction between Shogenji's measure and the C_3-measure given in Section 4 of this paper.

[6] I would like to thank an anonymous referee for helping to clarify the definition of prior independence.

[7] There seem to be two plausible values, 0 or 1, for $C_3(A,B)$ when $P(A \lor B) = 0$. The rationale for selecting the value of 0 is that the coherence measure generally yields a value of 0 when $P(A \land B) = 0$, which will be the case when $P(A \lor B) = 0$. The rationale for selecting the value of 1 is that the coherence of a belief with itself is 1 and even a contradictory belief could be considered to cohere maximally with itself.

[8] The idea of 'degree of overlap' becomes very clear if the probabilities of the beliefs are illustrated by a Venn diagram.

[9] Alternative responses to the problem of conjunction are presented by Shogenji (2001) and Olsson (2001).

[10] Other measures that are prior independent, deal adequately with deductive extremes and satisfy the Bovens–Olsson condition are $C_4(A,B) = 1/2 [P(A|B) + P(B|A)]$ and $C_5(A,B) = P(A|B) \times P(B|A)$.

REFERENCES

Akiba, K.: 2000, 'Shogenji's Probabilistic Measure of Coherence Is Incoherent', *Analysis* **60**, 356–359.

Bovens, L. and S. Hartmann: 2003, *Bayesian Epistemology*, Oxford University Press, Oxford.

Bovens, L. and E. J. Olsson: 2000, 'Coherentism, Reliability and Bayesian Networks', *Mind* **109**, 685–719.

Fitelson, B.: 2003, 'A Probabilistic Theory of Coherence', *Analysis* **63**, 194–199.

Glass, D. H.: 2002, 'Coherence, Explanation and Bayesian Networks', *Proceedings of the 13th Irish Conference in Artificial Intelligence and Cognitive Science,* edited by M. O'Neill et al., *Lecture Notes in AI 2646*, Springer-Verlag, New York, pp. 177–182.

Kemeny, J. G. and P. Oppenheim: 1952, 'Degrees of Factual Support', *Philosophy of Science* **19**, 307–324.

Olsson, E. J.: 2001, 'Why Coherence Is Not Truth-Conducive', *Analysis* **61**, 236–241.

Olsson, E. J.: 2002, 'What Is the Problem of Coherence and Truth?', *The Journal of Philosophy* **99**(5), 246–272.

Shogenji, T.: 1999, 'Is Coherence Truth-Conducive?', *Analysis* **59**, 338–345.

Shogenji, T.: 2001, 'Reply to Akiba on the Probabilistic Measure of Coherence', *Analysis* **61**, 147–150.

Siebel, M.: 2004, 'On Fitelson's Measure of Coherence', *Analysis* **64**, 189–190.

School of Computing and Mathematics
University of Ulster
Newtownabbey, Co. Antrim
BT37 0QB
U.K.
E-mail: dh.glass@ulster.ac.uk

Erkenntnis (2005) 63:387–412
DOI 10.1007/s10670-005-4007-z

ERIK J. OLSSON

THE IMPOSSIBILITY OF COHERENCE

ABSTRACT. There is an emerging consensus in the literature on probabilistic coherence that such coherence cannot be truth conducive unless the information sources providing the cohering information are individually credible and collectively independent. Furthermore, coherence can at best be truth conducive in a *ceteris paribus* sense. Bovens and Hartmann have argued that there cannot be any measure of coherence that is truth conducive even in this very weak sense. In this paper, I give an alternative impossibility proof. I provide a relatively detailed comparison of the two results, which turn out to be logically unrelated, and argue that my result answers a question raised by Bovens and Hartmann's study. Finally, I discuss the epistemological ramifications of these findings and try to make plausible that a shift to an explanatory framework such as Thagard's is unlikely to turn the impossibility into a possibility.

1. COHERENCE IN EPISTEMOLOGY

In ordinary life we usually rely on the information sources that we have at our disposal, placing our trust in the testimony of other people as well as in that of the senses. Such reliance, as a number of authors have pointed out, is automatic and routine.[1] This is most obvious for the testimony of the senses. Thus, I come to believe that my friend is over there as the direct effect of observing him without in any way inferring his presence from other beliefs I have. But the same is basically true of testimonies from other people. If the secretary tells me that my colleague was in his office just a moment ago, I simply believe it.

While the reception of testimony from various sources is normally unreflective, it is not thereby uncritical. Testimony is accepted so long as there is no explicit reason to doubt the credibility of the reporter, i.e., so long as certain trouble indicators are not present. For example, the information we receive from one source may contradict that received from another or we might have reasons to question the motives of our informant. Is she trying to deceive us? Even an informant with the best of intentions may turn out not to be trustworthy if there are signs that she acquired her information under problematic circumstances (e.g., under bad lighting conditions). If there are no special reasons for caution, the unreflective mechanism of reliance is invoked and one single testimony suffices to settle the matter, at least for the time being.[2]

Coherence becomes relevant once the reliability of our informants is, for some reason, in doubt, so that we are unable to take that which is being reported at face value. In this case it may pay off to listen to more than one source. If the sources cohere or agree to a large extent in their reporting we may conclude that what they say is true, even though this conclusion could not have been reached as the effect of listening to one of the sources only. If, for instance, the first dubious witness to be queried says that John was at the crime scene, the second that John has a gun and the third that John shortly after the robbery transferred a large sum to his bank account, then the striking coherence of the different testimonies would normally make us pretty confident, notwithstanding their individual dubiousness, that John is to be held responsible for the act.

Lewis made the same point when he asked us to consider a case of "relatively unreliable witnesses who independently tell the same circumstantial story" (1946, p. 246).[3]

For any one of these reports, taken singly, the extent to which it confirms what is reported may be slight. And antecedently, the probability of what is reported may also be small. But congruence of the reports establishes a high probability of what they agree upon.

The resulting probability of what is agreed need not merely be high but may even suffice for practical certainty:

Take the case of the unreliable observers who agree in what they report. In spite of the antecedent improbability of any item of such report, when taken separately, it may become practically certain, in a favourable case, merely through congruent relations to other such items, which would be similarly improbable when separately considered.

As Lewis makes clear, the foregoing remarks apply not only to witness reports but quite generally to "evidence having the character of 'reports' of one kind or other – reports of the senses, reports of memory, reports of other persons" (p. 347). Take, for instance, memory reports:

[S]omething I seem to remember as happening to me at the age of five may be of small credibility; but if a sufficient number of such seeming recollections hang together sufficiently well and are not incongruent with any other evidence, then it may become highly probable that what I recollect is fact. It becomes thus probable just in measure as this congruence would be unlikely on any other supposition which is plausible (p. 352).

Throughout, I will take "testimony" in the widest possible sense to include not only witness testimony but also, for instance, the "testimony of the senses" and the "testimony of memory".[4] Thus, I use "testimony" in the same sense in which Lewis uses "report".

The foregoing remarks are intended to highlight the *normal* use of coherence, i.e., its employment in inquiries characterized by (1) some of the warning signs being present making it inadvisable to accept testimonies at face value, but (2) there being nonetheless a substantial body of background assumption upon which we can, in fact, rely. Our background information, which is not in doubt in the context of the given inquiry, may tell us, for instance, that the informants are independent of each other and that they, while falling short of full reliability, are nonetheless to be regarded relatively reliable.

What is especially striking about coherence reasoning is that by combining items of information which are in themselves almost worthless one can arrive at a high probability of what is being reported. Indeed, it is salient how little knowledge of the reporters seems necessary for coherence to guarantee high likelihood of truth. We can, it seems, be *almost* entirely ignorant about the quality of our reporters and still arrive at practical certainty as the effect of observing their agreement. At least, this is what Lewis seems to suggest.

There is but a small step from arguing that coherence works under almost total ignorance to holding that it does so even if we remove "almost". If coherence is so successful in coping with context where *very little* is taken for granted, could it not also be invoked where *nothing* is? Hence the *anti-skeptical* use of coherence, i.e., the employment of coherence reasoning in skeptical contexts. These contexts are characterized by everything being called into question, except facts of a mere report character. The allowed reports typically state that a person believes or remembers this or that. The claim, then, is that a person can, using coherence reasoning, legitimately recover her trust in her beliefs or memories from this meager base. We can, it is contended, start off with literally nothing – as the skeptic insists – and yet, upon observing the coherence of our *de facto* memories or beliefs, conclude that those memories or beliefs are highly likely to be true.

Thus we are led to the kind of coherence theory advocated by Lewis and BonJour. Both intend to provide a final validation of our empirical knowledge through the anti-skeptical use of coherence reasoning on initially highly dubious data in the form of mere reports on what we believe or (seem to) remember. Their anti-skeptical theories are partly based on certain claims about what is supposed to be true of witness cases, typically accentuating the supposed success of coherence reasoning in such cases. These claims are then said to apply equally to various skeptical scenarios. A more recent example in the same vain is Coady's (1992) attempt to provide coherence justification of our trust in the testimony of others.

It is important to see that, in all the main epistemological applications of coherence, we are supposed to be presented with some sort of reports. That the reports are present is taken for granted. What is in doubt is whether the contents of the reports – beliefs contents, memory contents etc. – are true. To think otherwise – to think that coherence is to be applied to mere propositions that do not form the contents of some reports – is to commit what I call the *propositional fallacy*. To the best of my knowledge, there are no epistemological applications of coherence as applied to sets of mere propositions, as opposed to sets of reported propositions.

Following Klein and Warfield (1994, 1996), let us say that a measure of coherence is truth conducive if and only if more coherence implies a higher likelihood of truth. As a consequence of the foregoing observation, while it may be true that coherence is not truth conducive when applied to sets of mere propositions – as indeed Klein and Warfield argue – the philosophical relevance of this observation is highly questionable. The epistemologically relevant question is rather whether coherence is truth conducive when predicated of sets of reported propositions. As I have argued, in collaboration with Bovens, the kind of counterexamples to the truth conduciveness of coherence provided by Klein and Warfield have no bearing on the latter question (Bovens and Olsson, 2002).

As has also been argued in the literature – by myself and others – coherence is not truth conducive in the interesting sense unless the circumstances are, in certain respects, fortunate.[5] Thus we need to assume that the reports are collectively independent and individually credible (at least to some degree). Coherence has no effect on the likelihood of truth if the reporters have fudged their story into agreement. Independent reports that are useless when taken singly remain useless when combined, however mutually coherent their contents may be.

Another insight that is gaining acceptance is that coherence can be truth conducive at best in a *ceteris paribus* sense. The most we can hope for is for more coherence to imply higher likelihood of truth, *other things being equal* (Olsson, 2002a).

Let us say that a measure of coherence is *weakly truth conducive* if it is truth conducive *ceteris paribus* given individual credibility and collective independence. It is an open question in the literature whether there are any coherence measures that are weakly truth conducive. In this paper, I will attempt to show that there are no (non-trivial) measures of that kind.[6]

2. THE CONCEPT OF COHERENCE

The nature of coherence is very much an open question in the epistemological literature. The lack of a definite account of the central concept has been a constant source of embarrassment for coherence theorists. The aim of this paper is not to make a positive contribution in this direction. On the contrary, I intend to show why attempting to define coherence is futile. But in order to do so we must have some basic idea of what a coherence measure is supposed to be.

To avoid the propositional mistake, it is important to make sure that the notion of coherence not be applied to sets of mere propositions, but to sets of *reported* propositions. More precisely, coherence should be predicated of *testimonial systems*. A testimonial system is a set $\mathbf{S} = \{\langle E_1, H_1 \rangle, \langle E_2, H_2 \rangle, \ldots, \langle E_n, H_n \rangle\}$ where the E_is and H_is are propositions. Intuitively, E_i is a report to the effect that H_i is true. Thus, H_i can be thought of as the content of the report E_i.

We can define the degree of coherence of a testimonial system in two steps:

Step 1: Define degree of coherence for sequences of propositions.
Step 2: Define the degree of coherence of a testimonial system as the degree of coherence of the sequence of its content propositions.

How could we define the degree of coherence of sequences of propositions?[7] Before we take a look at two recent suggestions, it is natural to consider the following simple measure which equates the degree of coherence of a sequence with its joint probability:

$$C_0(H_1, \ldots, H_n) = P(H_1 \wedge \cdots \wedge H_n)$$

Hence, the more likely it is that the proposition are true together, the higher is their degree of coherence. While this may sound plausible at first, it is easy to see that it does not do justice to our intuitive concept of coherence. Suppose a crime has been committed, leaving us wondering who might have done it. Consider the following reports:

Witness no. 1: "Steve did it"
Witness no. 2: "Steve did it"
Witness no. 3: "Steve, Martin or David did it"
Witness no. 4: "Steve, John or James did it"

Which pair of reports would you consider more coherent – that of
the first two witness or that of the last two? Presumably, you would
favour the reports by the first two witnesses. In other words, you
would consider ⟨"Steve did it", "Steve did it"⟩ to be more coherent
than ⟨"Steve, Martin or David did it", "Steve, John or James did it"⟩.
After all, the first two reports are in perfect agreement, whereas the
latter two are not. The C_0 measure, on the other hand, rules that these
two pairs are equally coherent, as the joint probability of the one
equals the joint probability of the other.

This suggests that we need to measure the degree to which propositions agree. One way to measure agreement, proposed without
endorsement in Olsson (2002a) and independently in Glass (2002),
would be:

$$C_1(H_1, \ldots, H_n) = \frac{P(H_1 \wedge \cdots \wedge H_n)}{P(H_1 \vee \cdots \vee H_n)}$$

It is easy to see that this measure assigns a maximum coherence value
of 1 in all cases of full agreement.

Another way to quantify the degree of agreement is to divide the
joint probability not by the probability of the disjunction (as in C_1) but
by the product of the propositions' individual probabilities (Shogenji,
1999):[8]

$$C_2(H_1, \ldots, H_n) = \frac{P(H_1 \wedge \cdots \wedge H_n)}{P(H_1) \times \cdots \times P(H_n)}$$

The following example highlights the difference in outcome between applying C_1 and C_2. This time we focus on the following reports:

Witness no. 1: "Steve did it"
Witness no. 2: "Steve did it"
Witness no. 3: "Steve, Martin or David did it"
Witness no. 4: "Steve, Martin or David did it"

Again we ask ourselves which pair of reports exhibits a higher
degree of coherence – the first or the last. In this case, one may come
up with different answers depending on how one is reasoning. One
may, on the one hand, be inclined to say that the degree of coherence is
the same on the ground that they are both cases of full agreement. This
is also what C_1 dictates. Alternatively, one may be led to think that the
first pair is more coherent since what is agreed here is more specific.

This is also what C_2 rules. Thus, C_1 measures how well propositions agree, whereas C_2 measures how striking or salient the agreement is.

Again, the purpose of the foregoing discussion is not to establish anyone of these measures as the correct measure of coherence. Instead, they are just meant to illustrate what a coherence measure could look like. In general, we will mean by a (probabilistic) *coherence measure* any numerical measure that assigns to each sequence $\langle H_1,..., H_n \rangle$ of propositions a number $C(H_1,...,H_n)$ defined solely in terms of the probability of $H_1,...,H_n$ (and their Boolean combinations) and standard arithmetical operations. Clearly, C_0, C_1 and C_2 are all cases in point.

Given a measure of coherence for propositional sequences, we can now define the degree of coherence of a testimonial system. In accordance with what was said above, the degree of coherence of a testimonial system $\mathbf{S} = \{\langle E_1, H_1 \rangle, \langle E_2, H_2 \rangle,...,\langle E_n, H_n \rangle\}$ equals by definition the degree of coherence of $\langle H_1, H_2,..., H_n \rangle$. This captures the important idea that coherence is supposed to be a property at the level of report contents. Notation: $C_P(\mathbf{S})$ = the degree of coherence assigned to $\mathbf{S}$ by measure C relative to probability distribution P.

To take an example, let

H_1 = "John was at the crime scene"

H_2 = "John has a gun"

H_3 = "John had a motive"

The following is a testimonial system:

$\mathbf{S} = \{\langle$"Smith says that H_1", $H_1\rangle$,

$\quad\quad\langle$"Mary says that H_2", $H_2\rangle$,

$\quad\quad\langle$"Karen says that H_3", $H_3\rangle\}$

Moreover, $C(\mathbf{S}) = C(\langle H_1, H_2, H_3 \rangle) = C(H_1, H_2, H_3)$.

It is worth emphasizing that coherence, as conceived here, is not conceptually linked to reliability. Coherence is a phenomenon on the level of contents of reports, whereas reliability concerns the relation between a report and its content, i.e., how good a sign the former is of the latter. This is as it should be. We are supposed to be ignorant of the reliability of our data (memories, beliefs, witness reports,...), and so a notion of coherence that depended on reliability would be of little use in an argument against skepticism.

3. WEAK TRUTH CONDUCIVENESS

We are interested in whether there are coherence measures that are truth conducive in the weak sense. Is a more coherent testimonial system therefore likely to be true – at last in fortunate circumstances and in a *ceteris paribus* sense? It is time to spell out what such weak truth conduciveness really amounts to.

First of all: what is the likelihood of truth (probability) of a testimonial system $S = \{\langle E_1, H_1 \rangle,...,\langle E_n, H_n \rangle\}$? It is tempting to take that likelihood to be $P(H_1,...,H_n)$. This, however, would be quite inaccurate. As we have already noted, it can be assumed that the reports have actually been delivered, i.e., that $E_1,..., E_n$ are all true. Hence, $E_1,..., E_n$ are to be counted as evidence. The Principle of Total Evidence dictates that we should, when computing probabilities, take all available evidence into account. Hence, the *probability* of a testimonial system is $P(S) = P(H_1,..., H_n/E_1,..., E_n)$, i.e., the joint probability of the contents given the reports.[9] We will sometimes refer to $P(S)$ as the posterior probability and to $P(H_1,..., H_n)$ as the prior probability.

We can now define truth conduciveness in the following manner: a coherence measure C is *truth conducive* if and only if: if $C_P(S) > C_{P'}(S')$, then $P(S) > P'(S')$. In words: a coherence measure is truth conducive whenever more coherence means higher likelihood, regardless of how probabilities are assigned and regardless of what systems are compared. Why do we allow both the probability distribution and the testimonial system to vary between situations that are compared with respect to their relative degree of coherence? Well, why not? I am not aware of any reasons to keep the probability assessments fixed while varying only the testimonial system. By the same token, there seems to be no argument for fixing the testimonial systems while varying the probabilistic assumptions. In the absence of an argument to the contrary, it seems wise to be as liberal as possible in these regards.

How should we understand the "fortunate circumstances", more precisely? By individual credibility is simply meant positive relevance. Thus report E is credible if it raises the probability of its content H, i.e., if $P(H/E) > P(H)$. By collective independence we mean conditional independence in the standard sense. For the purposes of this paper, it will suffice to have that notion defined for the simple case of two reports E_1 and E_2 reporting the same proposition H. The assumption of conditional independence has two parts, corresponding to assuming H true or H false: $P(E_1/H) = P(E_1/H,E_2)$ and $P(E_1/\neg H) = P(E_1/\neg H, E_2)$. It is generally agreed that this notion of independence is adequate in this context and I refer to the literature for further motivation.[10]

Let us turn to the *ceteris paribus* clause. Why should such a clause be imposed in the first place? Suppose we are presented with two testimonial systems, one more coherent than the other. Then, whatever we mean by coherence more precisely, the less coherent (but consistent) system may still be more probable if its reports are individually more credible. In the limit case, the reports of the less coherent system are fully credible, raising the probability of their contents to 1. But it seems unfair to allow such deviations in individual credibility when evaluating the truth conduciveness of a given coherence measure. It seems that factors which have nothing to do with coherence should be kept fixed, especially if they are apt to influence the probability of a testimonial system. Individual credibility is precisely such a factor.

A more controversial issue is what else should be included in the *ceteris paribus* condition. In particular, should we require that the prior probability of the report contents remains fixed? I have argued outgoing from a general analysis of *ceteris paribus* conditions that it should not.[11] The reason is that the prior probability is, in a sense, not sufficiently separable from the degree of coherence. The C_2 measure, for instance, makes coherence heavily dependent on prior probability. Hence prior probability does not belong to the "other things" and so the *ceteris paribus* clause does not require that it remain equal. Individual credibility, by contrast, is separable from the degree of coherence. Changing the individual credibility does not change the degree of coherence.

4. AN IMPOSSIBILITY THEOREM

We are now in a position to address the main issue: are there any measures of coherence that are truth conducive *ceteris paribus* given independence and individual credibility? I will show that even in the simplest of cases there can be no coherence measure that is truth conducive in this weak sense.

We will consider a case of full agreement between independent reports that are individually credible, while respecting the *ceteris paribus* condition. We will show that there are no informative coherence measures that are truth conducive *ceteris paribus* in such a scenario which I will refer to as a *basic Lewis scenario*. The name is appropriate considering Lewis's reference to relatively unreliable witnesses telling the same story. A number of additional constraints will be imposed on the probabilities involved. The constraints are borrowed from a model proposed by Bovens et al. (2002). That model was in turn devised as an improvement of the model suggested in Olsson (2002b).[12] The most salient feature of this sort of model is that the reliability profile of the witnesses is, in a sense, incompletely known. The witnesses may be completely reliable (R) or they may be completely unreliable (U), and initially we do not know which possibility holds. An interesting consequence of this sort of model is that, from a certain context-dependent level of prior improbability, the posterior probability will be inversely related to the prior: the lower the prior, the higher the posterior. This feature is exploited in the following.

DEFINITION 1. A *basic Lewis scenario* is a pair $\langle S,P \rangle$ where $S = \{\langle E_1, H \rangle, \langle E_2, H \rangle\}$ and P a class of probability distributions defined on the algebra generated by propositions E_1, E_2, R_1, R_2, U_1, U_2 and H such that $P \in P$ if and only if:

(i) $P(R_i) + P(U_i) = 1$
(ii) $0 < P(H) < 1$
(iii) $P(E_1/H,R_1) = 1 = P(E_2/H,R_2)$
(iv) $P(E_1/\neg H, R_1) = 0 = P(E_2/\neg H, R_2)$
(v) $P(E_1/H,U_1) = P(H) = P(E_2/H,U_i)$
(vi) $P(E_1/\neg H, U_1) = P(H) = P(E_2/\neg H, U_2)$
(vii) $P(R_i/H) = P(R_i) = P(R_i/\neg H)$
(ix) $P(R_1) = P(R_2) > 0$

It can be shown that basic Lewis scenarios satisfy the conditions of individual credibility and independence.

LEMMA 1. (Theorem 3 in Bovens et al., 2002) Let $\langle S,P \rangle$ be a basic Lewis scenario. Letting $h = P(H), \bar{h} = P(\neg H)$ and $r = P(R_i)$, then

$$P(H/E_1, E_2) = h^* = \frac{(h + r\bar{h})^2}{h + r^2\bar{h}}$$

LEMMA 2. (Bovens et al., 2002, p. 547) Let $\langle S,P \rangle$ be a basic Lewis scenario. For all r, h^* as a function of h has a unique global minimum for $h \in \,]0,1[$ which is reached at

$$h_{\min} = \frac{r}{1 + r}$$

[104]

By calculating the first derivative one can see that h^* increases (decreases) strictly monotonically for $h > (<) h_{min}$.

Observation 1: $0 < h^* < 1$
Observation 2: $h^* \to 1$ as $h \to 0$
Observation 3: $h_{min} \to 0$ as $r \to 0$
Observation 4: $h_{min} \to \frac{1}{2}$ as $r \to 1$

DEFINITION 2. Let C be a coherence measure. C is *informative* in a basic Lewis scenario $\langle S,P \rangle$ if and only if there are P, $P' \in P$ such that $C_P(S) \neq C_{P'}(S)$.

DEFINITION 3. A coherence measure C is *truth conducive ceteris paribus* in a basic Lewis scenario $\langle S,P \rangle$ if and only if: if $C_P(S) > C_{P'}(S)$, then $P(S) > P'(S)$ for all $P,P' \in P$ such that $P(R_i) = P'(R_i)$.

The stipulation that $P(R_i) = P'(R_i)$ is part of the *ceteris paribus* condition. The other part, concerning independence, is guaranteed already by the fact that we are dealing with Lewis scenarios that, so to speak, have independence built into them.

I will make frequent use in the following of the fact that a probability distribution in P is uniquely characterized by the probability it assigns to H and R_i. Furthermore, for every pair $\langle r,h \rangle$ there is a probability distribution $P_{r,h}$ in P such that $P(R_i) = r$ and $P(H) = h$.

Observation 5: $P_{r,hmin(r)} (H/E_1,E_2) \to 0$ as $r \to 0$

THEOREM. There are no informative coherence measures that are truth conducive *ceteris paribus* in a basic Lewis scenario.
PROOF. We will seek to establish that if C is truth conducive *ceteris paribus* in a basic Lewis scenario, then C is not informative in such a scenario. We recall that the degree of coherence of an evidential system $S = \{\langle E_1, H \rangle, \langle E_2, H \rangle\}$ equals the coherence of the pair $\langle H,H \rangle$. Moreover, if C is a coherence measure then $C(\langle H,H \rangle)$ is defined in terms of the probability of H and its Boolean combinations, as explained in Section 2 above. In other words, $C_P(\langle H,H \rangle) = C(h)$ where $h = P(H)$. From what we just said it is clear that in order to show that C is not informative, in the sense of $C_P(S) = C_{P'}(S)$ for all $P,P' \in P$, it suffices to prove that $C(h)$ is constant for all $h \in]0,1[$. We will try to accomplish this in two steps, by first showing that $C(h)$ is constant in $I =]0,1/2[$ and then extending this result to the whole interval $]0,1[$. ∎

Suppose that C is not constant in I. Hence, there are $h_1, h_2 \in I$ such that $C(h_1) \neq C(h_2)$. We may assume $h_1 < h_2$.

CASE 1. $C(h_1) > C(h_2)$. By Observation 3, $h_{\min}$ goes to 0 as r goes to 0. Since $h_1 > 0$, it follows that there is a probability of reliability r such that $h_{\min} < h_1$. Consider distributions P_{r,h_1} and P_{r,h_2} in $\mathbf{P}$. By Lemma 2, $h_{\min}$ is a unique global minimum and h^* is monotonically decreasing for $h > h_{\min}$. Hence, $P_{r,h_1}(h_1/E_1, E_2) < P_{r,h_2}(h_2/E_1, E_2)$. Hence, C is not truth conducive (see Figure 1).

CASE 2. $C(h_1) > C(h_2)$. By Observation 4, $h_{\min}$ goes to 1/2 as r goes to 1. It follows that there is a probability of reliability r such that $h_2 < h_{\min} < 1/2$. Consider distributions P_{r,h_1} and P_{r,h_2} in $\mathbf{P}$. By Lemma 2, $h_{\min}$ is a unique global minimum and h^* is monotonically increasing for $h < h_{\min}$. Hence, $P_{r,h_1}(h_1/E_1, E_2) > P_{r,h_2}(h_2/E_1, E_2)$. It follows that C is not truth conducive (see Figure 2).

What has been shown so far is that, if C is truth conducive, C is constant in I.

We will proceed to show that, if C is truth conducive, then C is constant in $I' = [1/2, 1[$ as well. Suppose C is truth conducive but not constant in I'. Since C is truth conducive, $C(h) = c$ for all $h \in I$. Since C is assumed not constant in I', there is an $h \in I'$ such that $C(h) \neq c$.

CASE 1. $C(h) > c$. By Observation 2, $P_{r,h}(H/E_1, E_2)$ goes to 1 as h goes to 0. Since $P_{r,h}(H/E_1, E_2) < 1$, there is a $h' \in I$ such that $P_{r,h'}(H/E_1, E_2) > P_{r,h}(H/E_1, E_2)$, whereas $C(h') = c < C(h)$. This contradicts the assumption of C's truth conduciveness (see Figure 3).

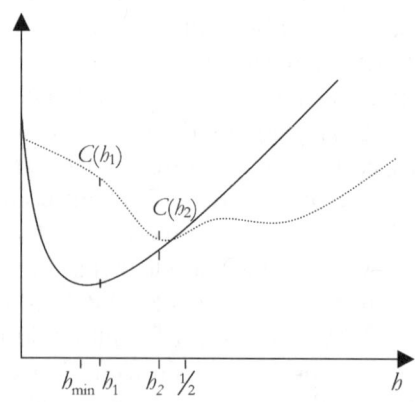

Figure 1. $C(h_1) > C(h_2)$. By choosing r such that $h_{\min} < h_1$ we can construct a counter example to the truth conduciveness of C in the interval $I =]0, 1/2[$.

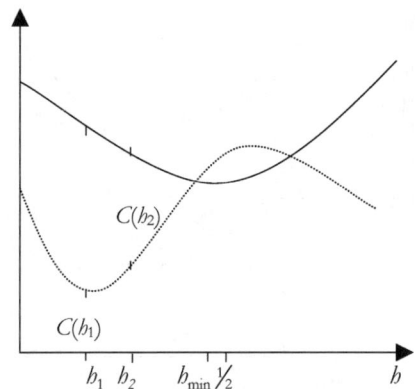

Figure 2. $C(h_1) < C(h_2)$. By choosing r such that $h_{\min} \in]h_2,1/2[$ we can construct a counter example to the truth conduciveness of C for $h \in]0,1/2[$.

CASE 2. $C(h) < c$. By Observation 5, $P_{r,h\min}(H/E_1,E_2)$ goes to 0 as r goes to 0. By Observation 3, $h_{\min}$ goes to 0 as r goes to 0. It follows by these two observations and the fact that $P(h) > 0$ that there is an r such that $P_{r,h\min}(H/E_1,E_2) < P_{r,h}(H/E_1,E_2)$ with $h_{\min} \in I$. Since $h_{\min} \in I$, $C(h_{\min}) = c > C(h)$. We have shown that there is an h' such that $C(h) < C(h')$ and yet $P_{r,h}(H/E_1, E_2) > P_{r,h'}(H/E_1, E_2)$. Again, we have a clash with the assumption that C is truth conducive (see Figure 4).

We have reached a contradiction and may conclude that, if C is truth conducive, then C is constant not only in I but also in I' so that C is in fact constant in the whole interval $]0,1[$. As we said at the beginning, this is sufficient to establish that, if C is truth conducive *ceteris paribus* for a basic Lewis scenario, then C is not informative in such a scenario QED.

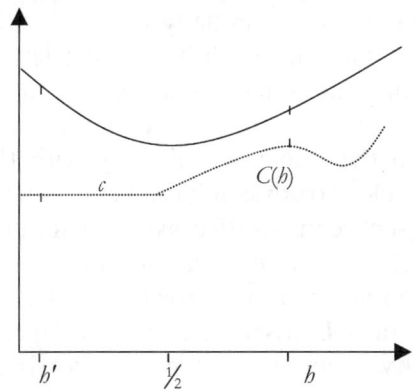

Figure 3. $C(h) > c$. There is then a point h' such that $C(h') = c < C(h)$ but $P_{r,h'}(H/E_1, E_2) > P_{r,h}(H/E_1, E_2)$.

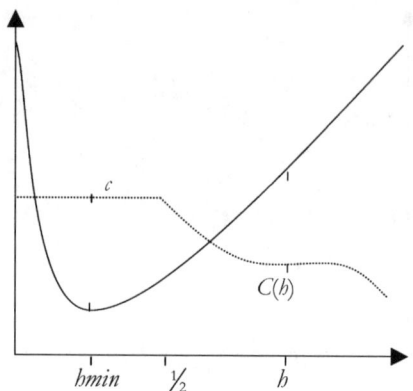

Figure 4. $C(h) < c$. By choosing r so that $P_{r,hmin}(H/E_1,E_2) < P_{r,h}(H/E_1,E_2)$ we get a counter example to the truth conduciveness of C.

5. DISCUSSION

What is it that drives this impossibility theorem? The crucial insight behind it is that exactly how the posterior varies with the prior in this sort of scenario depends not only on the prior probability of what the reports say (H), but also on the prior probability that those reports are reliable (R_i). We can get widely different posteriors depending on how we choose the probability of reliability and, what proves to be absolutely crucial here, the very *kind* of dependence of the prior on the posterior, i.e., the level of improbability at which agreement starts becoming a significant posterior-raising fact is contingent on the prior probability of reliability. In other words, where the curve for the posterior takes on its minimum value is contingent on how we assign the prior probability of reliability. The less probable we take it to be initially that the reports are reliable, the more that minimum will be shifted to the left (referring to the figures above). Thus, not only the absolute but also the *relative* height of the posterior, i.e. what is to count as more or less probable conditional on the evidence, will vary with the initial probability of reliability. Now truth conduciveness, as we have defined it, involves precisely such comparative assessments of posterior probability. Based on this observation alone one might be led to conjecture that there cannot be a non-trivial measure of coherence that is truth conducive in a Lewis type scenario; depending heavily on the precise reliability assumptions, the posterior is underdetermined by facts of coherence alone. What the theorem shows is that this conjecture is correct.

We observe that the degree of coherence in the case we are studying is a function of the prior probability of H. The trick is to show that any such function will, if it is informative, fail to be truth conducive. A counterexample can always be produced by varying the probability of reliability in a strategic way so as to falsify the claim that more coherence, according to the coherence function, implies a higher posterior probability of H. I will comment further on the theorem below in connection with a similar result by Bovens and Hartmann.

The theorem shows that a measure of coherence must pay a price for being truth conducive in a basic Lewis scenario. The price to pay is uninformativeness, i.e., the measure cannot make any distinctions as to coherence but must assign the same coherence value, regardless of the prior probability. The price is substantial since the posterior can vary greatly with the prior in a basic Lewis scenario. Thus, any truth conducive measure of coherence is necessarily useless in the assessment of the height of the posterior. Neither C_0 nor C_2 is uninformative in this sense. Both are heavily dependent on the prior probability of the report contents. This is obvious in the case of C_0 which *is* the prior probability of the report contents, but it is equally true of C_2. As the reader can verify, $C_2(H,H) = \frac{1}{H}$, that is to say, C_2 is inversely related to the prior in a Lewis set-up. Hence, neither C_0 nor C_2 is truth conducive in a basic Lewis scenario. By contrast, the theorem does not rule out the truth conduciveness of C_1. The reason, of course, is that C_1 is uninformative in a basic Lewis scenario, assigning as it does a coherence value of 1 independently of the prior probability of what is being agreed. The generality of the impossibility theorem should be clear. In order to be truth conducive a coherence measure must clearly be truth conducive in a basic Lewis scenario. But this, again, is not possible unless it is uninformative in such a scenario.

6. COMPARISON WITH BOVENS AND HARTMANN'S THEORY

I take the opportunity to comment on a new impossibility result by Bovens and Hartmann (2003) which is similar in spirit to the result proved here. Their result came to my knowledge as I was finalizing this paper, and I regret that I cannot give a full account of their substantial achievements.[13]

The upshot of their reasoning, too, is that it is impossible to define a general truth conducive measure of coherence, that is to say, they claim to have solved the problem that was first described in Olsson (2002a) as the remaining problem of coherence and truth. Another interesting feature of their book is their proposal for how the coherence theory of justification could be saved from their initial dialectical attack. The main idea is that while it is, in their view, impossible to define a truth conducive measure of coherence in a way that makes all sets comparable with regard to coherence, this is in fact not damaging to the coherence theory. The reason, they say, is that some sets are intuitively not comparable with regard to coherence. If this is true, then the impossibility may be an artifact resulting from attempting to compare what is actually incommensurable. The interesting question is whether there could be truth conducive coherence orderings of sets that are intuitively comparable. In the second chapter of their book, such a "quasi-ordering" is defined with much ingenuity and formal sophistication, and it is argued that it is indeed truth conducive.

One problem with the first two chapters of their book concerns the interpretation of Lewis, whom Bovens and Hartmann rightly refer to as a prominent advocate of the truth conduciveness of coherence. The impossibility result, which is at least initially presented as a problem for Lewis among others, is based on the assumption that the information sources are reliable to a certain, fixed degree which is not subject to change as more information arrives. This sort of reliability is called "exogenous" in the book. Lewis, on the other hand, was quite clear about the fact that in the kind of scenario he took interest in the reliability is initially uncertain and vulnerable to subsequent revision. In fact, I cannot think of any coherence theorist who has shown interest in exogenous reliability. What then, I asked myself, is the philosophical relevance of the impossibility theorem? The problem turned out to be one of presentation only. My question was answered in their third chapter where Bovens and Hartmann proceed to take the more complex situation with uncertain or "endogenous" reliability into account, arguing that their impossibility result can be generalized to cover that sort of case as well.

Here are some remarks on the relation between Bovens and Hartmann's theorem and mine.

Let us start with the question of what they have actually proved. In their argument, they refer to a situation involving three non-equivalent testimonies and two particular assignments of probabilities to the asserted propositions, showing that what probability assignment is associated with a higher posterior probability, i.e. joint probability given the evidence, depends on how reliable the sources

are. Since coherence is assumed to be reliability-independent, there is
no coherence measure that makes more coherence imply higher
posterior probability in the case at hand. From this, Bovens and
Hartmann draw the following conclusion: "we can conclude that
there cannot exist a measure of coherence that is probabilistic and
induces a coherence ordering for information triples ... and that
simultaneously makes it the case that the more coherent the information set, the more confident we are that the information is true,
ceteris paribus ..." (p. 21). Yet this does not follow from their
example. In fact, any measure that assigns the same coherence value
for both probability assignments would do the job. For any such
measure, more coherence would imply a higher likelihood of truth for
that particular assignment (be it in a trivial sense). Hence, Bovens and
Hartmann actually prove a weaker claim than they claim to have
proved. What they show is that there is no measure of coherence that
makes more coherence imply higher likelihood of truth *ceteris paribus*
(under certain fortunate circumstances) *and is informative for the two
particular probability assignments figuring in their example.* It is perfectly compatible with their result that there is a totally defined
coherence measure that is truth conducive so long as that measure
assigns an equal degree of coherence in problematic cases. There is
prima facie no need for a quasi-ordering. Maybe Bovens and Hartmann should have explored the more conservative strategy of
assigning problematic cases an equal degree of coherence before
embarking on the more radical path of declaring certain probability
assignments to information sets coherentistically incommensurable.

It is worth adding that Bovens and Hartmann have no argument
to the effect that it is impossible to define an informative coherence
measure that makes more coherence associated with a higher posterior given *any* two distinct assignments of probabilities to an
information set. In fact, they show, on p. 23 of their book, that there
are assignments for which their way of constructing counterexamples
does not work.

The most salient difference between Bovens and Hartmann's result
and mine is that I focus on a case of fully agreeing or, more generally,
equivalent testimonies. A second difference is that my argument does
not hinge on any particular assignment of probabilities to the asserted propositions. Rather, I prove that given *any* two distinct
assignments of probabilities to an information set (consisting of two
equivalent propositions) it is impossible to define an informative
coherence measure that makes more coherence associated with higher
posterior (where informativeness is relative to such a basic Lewis

scenario). This suggests, but does not establish, that my way of constructing counterexamples is more powerful than theirs. The trick is to vary the probability of reliability in ways affecting the relationship between posterior and prior probability of what is being asserted, which leads me to the final point of comparison: unlike Bovens and Hartmann's proof, mine is carried out in a scenario that involves endogenous reliability in an essential way; it is crucial to my proof that one can distinguish between two hypotheses regarding the reliability − full reliability and complete unreliability − so that one can meaningfully speak of a "probability of reliability".

It has been suggested to me that Bovens and Hartmann's result is more general than mine. It is true that they have a different conception of what is to be included among the ceteris paribus conditions. In their view, but not in mine, not only the degree of reliability but also the joint prior probability of an information set should be held fixed when comparisons as to coherence are made. Consequently, their aim is to show that coherence is not even truth conducive among information sets having the same prior joint probability, a condition that is satisfied in their example. Had they succeeded in doing this, there might have been a basis for arguing for the greater generality of their result. But, again, what they have proved is actually a weaker statement that involves a reference to the informativeness of the coherence measure relative to a pair of particular probability assignments to an information set (different from the information set figuring in my proof). As far as I can judge, the two results are not only different but indeed logically unrelated.

There is a sense in which my theorem answers an open question raised by Bovens and Hartmann's argument, which does not rule out the existence of measures that are truth conducive in a restricted sense of being correlated with truth for the particularly simple and basic case of equivalent testimonies. My proof shows that there are no such measures that are informative. Indeed, it shows that no such measure exists even if one restricts attention further to sets of equivalent testimonies *of the same size*. The matter, which turns out to be highly non-trivial, depends on the subtle ways in which the choice of a prior probability of reliability influences the relationship between the prior and the posterior probability of what is being asserted.

The urgency of the question of truth conduciveness for equivalent statements depends, at least to some extent, on what kind of application one has in mind. If one is concerned with coherence among witness statements, as legal theorists would typically be, the matter is clearly important because witnesses not only may but often do deliver equivalent statements. The same is arguably true of most everyday employments of coherence in situations involving possibly unreliable sources. In all these cases, equivalent statements are both possible and frequent. Moreover, the posterior probability can vary tremendously with the prior probability and the number of testimonies, thus making the coherence assessment of the posterior potentially an urgent matter. If we focus our attention on measures that assign the same degree of coherence to equivalent testimonies, as Bovens and Hartmann do, regardless of prior probability and number of testimonies, we have ruled out by definition the possibility of making a coherence assessment of the height of the posterior in such cases. From the point of view of legal and everyday coherence reasoning, there is therefore every reason *not* to focus on measures of this type.

The matter is more delicate if one is exclusively interested in the coherence of one single person's beliefs or memories, as the anti-skeptic typically is. The reason is that the relevant sets whose degrees of coherence are to be ascertained are normally assumed to consist of beliefs having non-equivalent contents. The fact that Bovens and Hartmann's result involves sets of non-equivalent statements makes it somewhat more appealing in this particular context. Having said this, I should remind the reader that, while Lewis and BonJour were both mainly interested in the issue of skepticism, reflection on witness coherence plays an important role in their anti-skeptical argumentation. Both consider witness agreement to be a paradigm case not only of the application of the concept of coherence but also of how coherence, in their view, is positively correlated with likelihood of truth.

Leaving the comparison of the results behind, I remain dissatisfied with the tenor of Bovens and Hartmann's discussion of Cartesian skepticism which conveys the impression that the weak (comparative) truth conduciveness claim upon which they focus is all that is needed for the purposes of a coherence theory of justification; and accordingly that the coherence theorists' sole mistake has been to focus unduly on measures of coherence that impose an ordering, as opposed to a quasi-ordering, on information sets (pp. 26–27). In reality, weak truth conduciveness does not exhaust the coherence theorist's conception of truth conduciveness. Bovens and Hartmann fail to mention that Lewis, for one, was very clear about the need for a more substantial connection between coherence and truth. Lewis thought that we cannot, as a matter of principle, know how reliable our memories are. What we can know is only that they are reliable to some positive degree, though without knowing what that degree is

(Olsson, 2002a; Olsson and Shogenji, 2004). These considerations led him to urge that, for the purposes of a coherence theory, a *high* degree of coherence must be taken to imply a *high* likelihood of truth, regardless of the actual positive degree of reliability of the sources; it is thus insufficient to establish the comparative claim that a *higher* degree of coherence implies a *higher* likelihood of truth. Bovens and Hartmann's introduction of quasi-orderings does little in the direction of establishing the more ambitious contention.

7. COMPARISON WITH THAGARD'S THEORY

An interesting question is whether the impossibility theorem relies in any essential way on the fact that we have been working in a *probabilistic* framework. Is the impossibility result merely an artifact of our modeling assumptions, or does it rather point to a general phenomenon that is independent of particular representations? My view is that the latter is true. The impossibility theorem shows that the likelihood of truth of a given system is seriously underdetermined by facts at the level of propositional contents. In particular, it is underdetermined by facts of coherence.

Thagard's interesting theory of "explanatory coherence" is often seen as a competitor to a probabilistic account of coherence, and it is therefore an interesting question whether it can avoid the problems. This is not the place for an extensive discussion of this rather vexed issue. Rather, I will confine myself to noting, first, that Thagard seems to fall prey to the propositional fallacy. Second, Thagard's meticulous comparison between his own model and the probabilistic setting reveals that these frameworks are in principle very similar – perhaps more so than has been generally appreciated. This gives a *prima facie* reason to believe that a shift to the explanatory framework would not by itself block the impossibility. Third, Thagard himself raises serious doubts as to whether it is possible to measure the degree of coherence of a system, although he does so on grounds that seem different from those upon which our negative conclusion relies.[14]

Let us see how Thagard's theory works. What we begin with is, in the epistemological case, a set of propositions. They can cohere (fit together) or incohere (resist fitting together). Coherence relations include relations of explanation and deduction, whereas incoherence relations include different types of incompatibility, such as logical inconsistency. If two propositions cohere, there is a positive constraint between them. If they incohere, this gives rise to a negative constraint. The propositions are to be divided into ones that are accepted and ones that are rejected. A positive constraint between two propositions can be satisfied either by accepting both or by rejecting both. Satisfying a negative condition means accepting the one proposition while rejecting the other. A coherence problem, according to Thagard, consists in dividing a set of propositions into accepted and rejected in such a way that the most constraints are satisfied. Thagard presents several different computational models for solving coherence problems, including a model that is based on neural networks.

How different is Thagard's account of coherence from the conception that I have tried to shed light on? As I understand it, coherence is a property of a testimonial system. A testimonial system, we recall, is a set of pairs $\{\langle E_1, H_1 \rangle, ..., \langle E_n, H_n \rangle\}$ where E_i constitutes testimonial evidence for H_i. The evidence can, for instance, come in the form of testimony from other people, from memory or from the senses. In the Lewis–BonJour tradition, as I reconstruct it, coherence is applied only to structures of this general kind. Lewis, for example, tended to focus on coherence among a person's own memories. It is true that such coherence can raise the probability of other propositions of a purely hypothetical nature, e.g., the hypothesis that the evidence is reliably reported. But this is quite possible without any assessment of the "explanatory coherence" of the hypotheses with the evidence ever taking place. Of course, we could say that in such cases the hypotheses is coherent with the data, and Lewis sometimes adopted this manner of speaking. But I fail to see the point in so doing. Thagard's conception is different from the Lewis–BonJour theory since, in his theory, there are no constraints on what sort of proposition can figure in a coherence problem and hence no restriction on what sets of propositions can "cohere". Sets of propositions in a network will not in general be describable as testimonial systems. Typically, some propositions will have the status of evidence and others the status of (mere) hypotheses that were devised only to explain the evidence. For this reason, it is not clear to me how Thagard avoids the propositional fallacy – if indeed he does avoid it.

Just how different is Thagard's explanationist framework from the probabilistic setting adopted here? The upshot of his admirably detailed comparison of the two frameworks is that it is non-trivial but possible, at least in principle, to translate between the frameworks which is why "it is an open question whether explanationist or probabilist accounts are superior" (p. 271). Given the translatability between frameworks, one could conjecture that what holds in one framework should hold in the other. In particular, one could conjecture that what is impossible in the probabilistic framework − e.g. defining an interesting measure of coherence that is truth conducive in the weak sense − is just as impossible in Thagard's explanatory framework.

As to my third point, Thagard seems to agree that it is impossible to define a measure of degree of coherence. Having raised the issue, he makes the following observation:

> It would be desirable to define, within the abstract model of coherence as constraint satisfaction, a measure of the degree of coherence of a particular element [with the rest] or of a subset of elements, but it is not clear how to do so. Such coherence is highly nonlinear, since the coherence of an element depends on the coherence of all the elements that constrain it, including elements with which it competes. The coherence of a set of elements is not simply the sum of the weights of the constraints satisfied by accepting them, but depends also on the comparative degree of constraint satisfaction of other elements that negatively constrain them (p. 39).

Thagard goes on to say that his observation cast doubts also on the possibility of quantifying statements such as "Darwin's theory of evolution is more coherent than creationism". Thagard's conclusion is strikingly similar to our own negative results, although the exact relation between his reasons for drawing this conclusion and ours remains an open question.

8. ON THE FUTILITY OF ATTEMPTS TO DEFINE COHERENCE

In a recent paper, BonJour complains that "the precise nature of coherence remains an unsolved problem" (1999, p. 123). He proceeds:

> Spelling out the details of this idea in a way that would allow reasonably precise assessments of comparative coherence, is extremely difficult, at least partly because such an account will dependent on the correct account of a number of more specific and still inadequately understood topics, such as induction, confirmation, probability, explanation and various issues in logic ... (ibid.).

Long before BonJour voiced his doubts, Ewing wrote:

> I think, however, that it is wrong to tie down the advocates of the coherence theory to a precise definition. What they are doing is to describe an ideal that has never yet been completely clarified but is none the less immanent in all our thinking. It would be altogether unreasonable to demand that the moral ideal should be exhaustively defined in a few words, and the same may be true of the ideal of thought. As with the moral ideal, it may well be here that while formulae are helpful, they can provide no

complete stereotyped account, and the only adequate approach is one for which there is no space in this book, namely, a study of what our thought can do at its best by means of numerous examples (1934, p. 231).

Ewing is here suggesting that it might be impossible to capture the concept of coherence in a formula. But what sort of possibility are we talking about here? On a "weak" reading, Ewing is saying merely that it would be *practically* impossible, or at least difficult, to state a definition of coherence, as it would require more than "a few words". On this interpretation there is little difference in principle between Ewing's view and doubts later raised by BonJour.

Yet, Ewing's remarks also admit a stronger reading. Thus rendered, he is claiming, more radically, that defining coherence is *logically* impossible, that there is no formula or statement, however long, which could do the job adequately. Understood in this way, he is maintaining that there is no systematic account of coherence.

The main result of this paper can be seen as a vindication of Ewing's thesis *under the strong reading*. For it has been shown not only that it is impractical or difficult to define coherence, due to the length of formulas that would be required or to our lack of understanding of crucial notions which such a definition would have to refer to; the impossibility theorem shows that it is outright logically impossible to device such a definition.

There is no mystery about this result. In particular, it does not mean that coherence, while being comprehensible to the human intellect, somehow transcends rational definition. It means simply that the constraints that have been imposed, explicitly or implicitly, on such a definition are jointly incompatible. These constraints include, notoriously, the requirement that a definition of coherence should make that notion, in favourable circumstances, come out as truth conducive *ceteris paribus*. While having coherence imply truth might be too much to ask for, it should at least fall out of a suitable definition that more coherence implies higher probability in a weak *ceteris paribus* sense in favourable circumstances (independence, individual credibility). The constraints also include a condition of informativeness: the degree of coherence should give us some information about how high the posterior is, be it only information about its relative height. The whole point, after all, is to use coherence to assess the likelihood of truth in the face of our supposed initial ignorance about facts of reliability. I have argued that there can be no measure satisfying these requirements. Just as there are no square circles, there is nothing out there that could play the role coherence is supposed to play. The description of that role is itself incoherent. Small wonder, then, that there has been so little progress in defining coherence.

ACKNOWLEDGEMENTS

I would like to thank Mark Siebel and Staffan Angere for their helpful comments on an earlier version.

NOTES

[1] See, for example, Levi (1991) and Coady (1992). See also Olsson (2003) and Levi (2003).

[2] Cf. Coady (1992), p. 47: "We may have 'no reason to doubt' another's communication even when there is no question of our being gullible; we may simply recognize that the standard warning signs of deceit, confusion, and mistake are not present. This recognition incorporates our knowledge of the witness's competence, of the circumstances surrounding his utterance, of his honesty, of the consistency of the parts of his testimony, and its relation to what others have said, or not said, on the matter."

[3] All references to Lewis concern his 1946 essay *Knowledge and Valuation*.

[4] For an account of different senses of "testimony", including its use in legal contexts, see Chapter 2 in Coady (1992).

[5] Huemer (1997), Bovens and Olsson (2000), Olsson (2001, 2002a) and Olsson and Shogenji (2004).

[6] For a more detailed critique of the Lewis–BonJour tradition of thought, see Olsson (2005).

[7] This section is based on Olsson (2002a).

[8] For a longer discussion of this measure, see Olsson (2001).

[9] Compare Cross (1999).

[10] See Cohen (1977), Jeffrey (1987), Huemer (1997), Bovens and Olsson (2000), Olsson (2002a), Olsson and Shogenji (2004), and Olsson (2005).

[11] See Shogenji (1999) and Olsson (2001). Olsson (2002a) contains a detailed analysis of the *ceteris paribus* clause.

[12] For a discussion of the difference between the two models, see also Olsson (2002c).

[13] Although the book by Bovens and Hartmann which I am here concerned with is listed as published in 2003, it did not in fact appear until mid-2004.

[14] All references to Thagard concern his book from year 2000. For another version of an explanatory coherence theory, see Bartelborth (1996).

REFERENCES

Bartelborth, T.: 1996, *Begründungsstrategien: ein Weg durch die analytische Erkenntnistheorie*, Akademie Verlag, Berlin.

Bonjour, L.: 1985, *The Structure of Empirical Knowledge*, Harvard University Press, Cambridge, Mass.

Bonjour, L.: 1999, 'The Dialectics of Foundationalism and Coherentism', in J. Greco & E. Sosa (eds.), *The Blackwell Guide to Epistemology*, Blackwell, Malden, Mass., 117–142.

Bovens, L., B. Fitelson, S. Hartmann and J. Snyder: 2002, 'Too Odd (not) to Be True: A Reply to Erik J. Olsson', *British Journal for the Philosophy of Science* **53**, 539–563.

Bovens, L. and S. Hartmann: 2003, *Bayesian Epistemology*, Oxford University Press, Oxford.

Bovens, L. and E. J. Olsson: 2000, 'Coherentism, Reliability and Bayesian Networks', *Mind* **109**, 685–719.

Coady, C. A. J.: 1992, *Testimony: A Philosophical Study*, Clarendon Press, Oxford.

Cohen, L. J.: 1977, *The Probable and the Provable*, Clarendon Press, Oxford.

Cross, C. B.: 1999, 'Coherence and Truth Conducive Justification', *Analysis* **59**, 186–193.

Ewing, A. C.: 1934, *Idealism: A Critical Survey*, Methuen, London.

Glass, D. H.: 2002, 'Coherence, Explanation and Bayesian Networks', in *Proceedings of the Irish Conference in AI and Cognitive Science*, Lecture Notes in AI **2646**, Springer, New York, pp. 256–259.

Huemer, M.: 1997, 'Probability and Coherence Justification', *Southern Journal of Philosophy* **35**, 463–472.

Jeffrey, R.: 1987, 'Alias Smith and Jones: The Testimony of the Senses', *Erkenntnis* **26**, 391–399.

Klein, P. and T. A. Warfield: 1994, 'What Price Coherence?', *Analysis* **54**, 129–132.

Klein, P. and T. A. Warfield: 1996, 'No Help For the Coherentist', *Analysis* **56**, 118–121.

Levi, I.: 1991, *The Fixation of Belief and Its Undoing*, Cambridge University Press, Cambridge.

Levi, I.: 2003, 'Contracting from Epistemic Hell Is Routine', *Synthese* **135**, 141–164.

Lewis, C. I.: 1946, *An Analysis of Knowledge and Valuation*, Open Court, LaSalle.

Olsson, E. J.: 2001, 'Why Coherence Is not Truth-Conducive', *Analysis* **61**, 236–241.

Olsson, E. J.: 2002a, 'What Is the Problem of Coherence and Truth?', *The Journal of Philosophy* **99**, 246–272.

Olsson, E. J.: 2002b, 'Corroborating Testimony, Probability and Surprise', *British Journal for the Philosophy of Science* **53**, 273–288.

Olsson, E. J.: 2002c, 'Corroborating Testimony and Ignorance: A Reply to Bovens, Fitelson, Hartmann and Snyder', *British Journal for the Philosophy of Science* **53**, 565–572.

Olsson, E. J.: 2003, 'Avoiding Epistemic Hell: Levion Pragmatism and Inconsistency', *Synthese* **135**, 119–140.

Olsson, E. J.: 2005, *Against Coherence: Truth, Probability, and Justification*, Oxford University Press, Oxford.

Olsson, E. J. and T. Shogenji: 2004, 'Can We Trust Our Memories? C. I. Lewis's Coherence Argument', *Synthese* **142**, 21–41.

Shogenji, T.: 1999, 'Is Coherence Truth-Conducive?', *Analysis* **59**, 338–345.
Thagard, P.: 2000, *Coherence in Thought and Action*, MIT Press, Cambridge, Mass.

Department of Philosophy
Lund University, Kungshuset
SE-222 22, Lund
Sweden
E-mail: Erik_J.Olsson@fil.lu.se

Erkenntnis (2005) 63:413–423
DOI 10.1007/s10670-005-4003-3

KEITH LEHRER

COHERENCE AND THE TRUTH CONNECTION

ABSTRACT. There is an objection to coherence theories of knowledge to the effect that coherence is not connected with truth, so that when coherence leads to truth this is just a matter of luck. Coherence theories embrace falliblism, to be sure, but that does not sustain the objection. Coherence is connected with truth by principles of justified acceptance that explain the connection between coherence and truth. Coherence is connected with truth by explanatory principle, not just luck.

1. INTRODUCTION

There is a perennial challenge to coherence theories of knowledge. It is that coherence is not or might not be connected with truth in a way that yields knowledge. Let me attempt to articulate the objection in the most telling way and then explain why and how the kind of coherence theory I have articulated meets the challenge.[1] So what exactly is the challenge concerning coherence theories of knowledge and the truth connection? The challenge rests on the assumption that coherence results from a relationship between internal states of the subject, beliefs, for example, if coherence is a relationship between beliefs. A coherence theory need not claim that coherence is a relationship among beliefs. It might be a relationship between other states, for example, among representational states that differ from belief. The states might be less than beliefs, when it seems to one that something is the case or one has the impression that something is the case, even though one has doubts that stand in the way of believing what seems to be the case. On the other hand, the states might be more than belief, the positive evaluation and acceptance of beliefs and impressions, for example. It has even been suggested that states that are not representational, mere sensations, for example, might be components in systematic coherence and necessary to yield coherence. I am willing to admit any representational states might be a component, but I am unwilling to admit that nonrepresentational states are components or terms of the coherence relation when they are not represented. My reason is that unrepresented states, though they have a causal influence on the existence of representational states, lack features essential to terms of the coherence relation. It is only states that tells us something and have some content, that cohere with other states or conflict with other states. This assumption that the terms of coherence are representational states will not play any critical role in my response to the challenge, however. The response is consistent with a broader conception of coherence. Those who put forth the objection concerning the truth connection formulate it as an objection against notions of coherence that construe the coherence as a relation between representational or doxastic states, however. So the assumption that the terms of the coherence relation are representational state provides a formulation that directly confronts the challenge.

2. THE TRUTH CONNECTION CHALLENGE

The challenge involves a number of claims. The first claim is that however the representational states, beliefs, for example, are related to each other, no conclusion about the truth of any belief follows from the relationship of coherence between the internal states. This is the basic truth connection challenge. Take beliefs as the representational states that cohere with each other. It does not follow from the relationship between the beliefs, the challenge runs, that any of the beliefs are true, or, for that matter, likely to be true. So, there is no logical connection between coherence among beliefs and the truth of any of the cohering beliefs. There is no deduction from the premise of coherence to the truth of the conclusion of what is believed.

3. OBVIOUS REPLIES AND RESPONSES

Now there are some obvious replies to this objection. One is that coherence might be a relationship among beliefs that has truth as a constituent of it. For example, suppose someone defined coherence as a relationship of mutual support among beliefs that are true. In that case, it would follow that beliefs that cohere with each other are true. How would the challenger respond? The usual response is that coherence must be an internal relationship or it will not be accessible to the subject, that is, it will be as difficult to determine whether beliefs cohere as it is to determine whether they are true. That way of putting the challenge begs the question. The claim about the difficulty of determining whether beliefs cohere is equivalent to a claim about the difficulty of knowing whether the beliefs cohere. The coherence theorist claims that coherence yields knowledge. As the coherence theorist sees the matter, the challenge amounts to the claim that it is as difficult to know that beliefs cohere as to know that they are true. That claim is an obvious consequence of his theory that knowledge is coherence, however, rather than a cogent objection to it.

The point to notice is that whatever internal aspects or constituents coherence may possess, attacking the coherence theory because it fails to yield truth on the grounds that the coherence relationship must be an exclusively internal relationship among internal states is to attack straw. No coherence theorist who holds that truth is a condition of knowledge, which most do, will advocate the an internal relationship between internal states is sufficient for knowledge. Moreover, the influence of the Gettier problem (Gettier, 1963) on the literature will lead an advocate of a coherence theory to hold that it is not just the truth of the target belief that is necessary for knowledge but also the truth of beliefs that play a role in the justification of the belief.

4. THE GETTIER PROBLEM AND FALLIBLE JUSTIFICATION

The fact of the matter is that it was the Gettier problem that made it clear that the most critical objection to the coherence theories of knowledge was, in fact, an objection that all theories of knowledge must meet. The objection is that whatever sort of justification we have for believing what we do may coincide with the belief being true and yet fall short of knowledge. The basic reason is that the justification one has for believing what one does, indeed, for believing that it is true, might coincide with the truth of the belief in a way that is just luck. The basic idea is that justification may fail to provide a suitable truth connection. The formulation of the Gettier problem rested on an assumption that I am confident is correct, namely, that our justification for our beliefs is fallible, that is, we may be justified in believing something to be true that is, in fact, false. For the structure of the Gettier counterexample to the analysis of knowledge as justified true belief rested on the assumption that a person could be justified in believing something that is, in fact, false. The Gettier argument ran from a premise assuming that a person was justified in believing that p, where p was false, to the premise that the person deduced q from p, where q was true, to arrive at the Gettier conclusion that a person had a justified true belief, that q, that was not knowledge because it was arrived at by deduction from a false, though justified, belief (Gettier, 1963).

Now if we accept the Gettier assumption, which was neutral with respect to the nature of justification, assuming only that it was fallible, then we can see that a problem about a truth connection arises for any theory of justification that allows that justification is fallible. The problem is that if justification is fallible, then, even if a justified belief turns out to be true, the justification might not be connected with the truth of the belief in a way that converts to knowledge. Thus, the alleged defect of a coherence theory of knowledge, that coherence, and the justification consisting of coherence, might not be connected with the truth of a belief in a way that yields knowledge, is a general problem for all theories of fallible justification of whatever kind.

The truth connection problem arises for all theories of fallible justification that attempt to analyze knowledge in terms of justified true belief. Some additional condition is required because of the insufficiency of justified true belief for knowledge. Hence the long quest for the needed fourth condition of knowledge. It is not the purpose of this paper to add another attempt to the various and illuminating conditions that others have offered. It is to clarify the underlying nature of the problem and to suggest that the coherence theory is what is needed to solve the problem.

5. THE GETTIER PROBLEM EXPLAINED

The most important step toward solving the problem is to understand it. Take the most common form of the example (Lehrer, 1965). I have very strong evidence that a student in my class, Mr. Nogot, owns a Ferrari. He drives one, says that he owns one, perhaps showed me the purchase papers in a mood of enthusiasm, and all my evidence indicates that he owns a Ferrari. As it happens, perhaps through deception, perhaps through a legal glitch, he does not own the Ferrari. Suppose someone asks me if anyone in my class owns a Ferrari. I conclude, with justification, that someone in my class owns a Ferrari from my justified belief that Mr. Nogot owns a Ferrari. But he does not. However, and this is the important twist, it turns out that another student in my class, Mr. Havit, owns a Ferrari. I am entirely ignorant of this having only dealt with Mr. Havit in class concerning academic matters. So, I have justified true belief that someone in my class owns a Ferrari. The belief is justified, because I am justified in believing Mr. Nogot owns one, which he does not. It is true because Mr. Havit owns one, which is something that I do not even believe. So, I do not know that someone in my class owns a Ferrari.

Why don't I know exactly? There are many answers, but the one that is common to the various examples, is that my justification based on evidence concerning Mr. Nogot does not explain why my belief is true. Therefore, as far as my evidence is concerned, it is just a matter of luck that my belief that someone in my class owns a Ferrari turns out to be true. Why is it just a matter of luck? It is because there is no connection between the true premises of my justification, that Mr. Nogot drives a Ferrari, that he says he owns the car, that he showed me purchase papers concerning the Ferrari, that he is in my class, and the truth of the conclusion that someone in my class owns a Ferrari. My believing these premises and reasoning from them does not explain why I turn out to have a true belief.

The point needs refinement. It is, after all, possible that there is some connection between the truth of the premises and the truth of the conclusion. Suppose that Mr. Havit and Mr. Nogot thought it would be amusing to deceive a well-known epistemologist in an amusing way. So Mr. Havit loaned his Ferrari to Mr. Nogot, and then the events described above took place. Mr. Havit got Miss. Inquisitive to ask me if anyone in my class owns a Ferrari and when I answered in the affirmative, the team of Mr. Nogot, Mr. Havit and Miss. Inquisitive thought, "Gotcha" They smiled concluding that Lehrer has a justified true belief that someone in the class owns a Ferrari, but he does not know that someone in the class owns a Ferrari. So the Gotcha team, or the Gettier team, has won their point.

But why in this case do I lack knowledge? Is it just luck that my belief is true? Is there no connection between the truth of the premises I believe about Mr. Nogot and the conclusion that someone in my class owns a Ferrari? Miss Inquisitive, who is a party to it all, might say that the premises I believe about Mr. Nogot are true because Mr. Havit and Nogot arranged for me to believe in their truth in order to get me to believe something else that is true, namely, that someone in my class owns a Ferrari. So there is a truth connection between the truth of my premises and the truth of the conclusion. Moreover, it is not just luck that the conclusion I believe, that someone in my class owns a Ferrari, is true, it is the result of skillful deception. Yet I still do not know that conclusion is true, even though there is a truth connection, and even though it is deception and not luck that my belief is true.

What are we to say to this reply? Some, committed to externalism, might be inclined to reply that in the case of the deception I am deceived in such a way that I know. The information is transmitted in a deviant manner, to be sure, but knowledge transmitted from one person, Mr.Havit, through others, Mr. Nogot, remains knowledge even though the form of transmission is through deception. This externalist reply like other externalist replies fails as an adequate account of the difference between knowledge and belief.

6. EXPLANATION OF LUCK

From the point of view of the teacher, myself, in this case, there is no difference between the original case in which there is no connection between Mr. Nogot and Mr. Havit, and the case in which they conspire. The connection between his evidence, his true beliefs about Nogot, and his true belief that someone in his class owns a Ferrari is doxastically opaque. Moreover, given his beliefs, he would not conclude that someone in his class owns a Ferrari if he believed that Mr. Nogot did not own a Ferrari. Moreover, he would conclude that if his belief that someone in class owns a Ferrari turns out to be true even though Mr. Nogot does not own a Ferrari, then his belief is true as a matter of luck. Moreover, and most crucially, that conviction that it would be luck is a result of belief that he has about a truth connection that would, if correct, explain the truth of his conclusion. For he believes that someone in his class owns a Ferrari because Mr. Nogot who is in his class owns a Ferrari. It is the supposed truth of, "Mr. Nogot who is in my class owns a Ferrari," that explains the truth of, "Someone in my class owns a Ferrari," on his view of the matter. Failing that explanation, he lacks any explanation for the truth of the conclusion. So, failing that explanation of the truth connection, it would be luck if he turned out to be right in his conclusion even if someone else insured that he was in luck.

The relevance of these observations to the coherence theory is simple and direct. The coherence theory, as I conceive of it, is one that analyzes coherence in terms of the way in which what one believes or accepts meets the objections to a target belief or acceptance[2]. Now one objection, perhaps the most salient to what one accepts, is that there is no truth connection that explains why the evidence and justification one has leads to truth. Put in the positive mode, what one accepts contains an account of a truth connection to avoid the result that what one accepts is true as a matter of luck.

7. COHERENCE CONTAINS THE TRUTH CONNECTION

The explanation of how the coherence theory avoids the problem of the truth connection raised by Gettier is relatively straight-forward. Coherence, which is a form of justification consisting of the capacity of background systems of subjective states, such as acceptances, preferences concerning acceptances and reasonings, to defend a target acceptance against objections to it. Coherence is systematic defensibility, and defensibility is justification. However, the defense of a target acceptance requires meeting the objection that even if it turns out to be true, that is just a matter of luck. For there is no explanation of the connection between the background system and the truth of the target acceptance. So, for a target acceptance to cohere with the background system in a way that provides a defense or justification of it, the background system must contain a defense against the objection that the target acceptance, if true, is so as a matter of luck because the truth of the target acceptance is not explained by a truth connection between the background acceptance system and the truth of the target acceptance.

The preceding point explains the fundamental defect of externalism as a theory of knowledge and poses a problem. The defect is that external relationships, casual chains, reliable processes, nomological connections, though necessary for knowledge in some instances of acceptance, namely, those in which the absence of such relations constitutes an objection to the target acceptance, are not sufficient to convert acceptance or belief to knowledge. The reason is that such relations might be opaque to the subject, and, therefore, the subject cannot defend the target acceptance against the objections that the relationships do not exist. In short, then, an internal conception of the relationships is necessary for the conversion to knowledge.

8. OBJECTION: AN UNEXPLAINED TRUTH CONNECTION

This observation leads to an important objection to the project of the coherence theorist. The project is to provide enough content to the background system so that the truth of a target acceptance is explained by a truth connection from the point of view of the subject of the target acceptance. But now the problem arises that the explanation by the background system of the truth of a target acceptance must itself be true. The explanation of the truth of the materials of the background system is needed for the explanation to succeed. False premises of explanation reduce the explanation to illusion, to false explanation at best, when true explanation is what is required. Thus the objection is that the truth of the explaining principles is assumed, and, when assumed, unexplained. Thus, the coherence theory of justification and knowledge rests on an unexplained truth connection and the acceptance of it.

We do want to distinguish between justification and coherence on the one hand and truth and knowledge on the other. We have learned that from Gettier and falliblism. The objective of the coherence theorist is to so construe coherence that when the truth of what is accepted is added to coherence among what is accepted, including the premises needed for defense of a target claim, knowledge results. But now we seem to be confronted with another challenge. The acceptance of the truth connection needed to explain why the truth of the accepted target claim is not just luck must not itself turn out to be true just as a matter of luck. The acceptance of the truth connection itself is infected with the original problem. If it coheres with the system, the truth of the acceptance of the truth connection is luck and unexplained by a truth connection. In short, we seem to have arrived once again at the problem of an unexplained explainer.

9. THE PROBLEM OF LUCK IN TRUTH PARADISE

The problem can be intensified. On the one side, we have a subjective system, a system of acceptances or beliefs, and on the other side we have a system of truth. Now we might hold that if there is an adequate match between what we accept, on the subjective side, and what is true, on the other side, then that will be good enough to avoid Gettier problems. Since these problems always rest on some false proposition defeating the conversion of justification to knowledge, we shall have solved the problem about the truth connection if we require that the justification be undefeated. But then the objection comes forward and confronts the coherence theory with the original problem of the truth connection for the system, the truth connection writ large. Simply put it this. Assume that we are so fortunate that, though we are fallible, we are totally successful. Everything we accept is true. Every defense of every target acceptance is true. We are in the land of truth paradise. But is not our location just a matter of luck? We accept what we do and explain the truth connection of particular conclusion to particular premise by appeal to what is true. Moreover, if what we accept is true, as it would be in truth paradise, then we can say that the truth of the particular conclusion is not just a matter of luck but is explained. That looks good. But when we look at the entire system of acceptance and the truth of what is contained therein, it appears as though the truth of what we accept is a matter of luck within in the entire system, and the truth connection is itself just luck.

10. HOW A PRINCIPLE OF TRUTH CONNECTION IS EXPLAINED

The answer to the problem is to notice that there is no constraint on how general the explanation of the truth connection can be. The solution to the problem is, in outline, perfectly simple. The background system can contain a principle that explains the truth connection between any components of that subjective system and the truth of them. Moreover, on the assumption that the principle of explanation is true, the connection between the acceptance of the principle and the truth of the principle can be explained by the principle itself. That would require that the principle, as a principle of explanation, applies to the relationship between the coherence of the principle within the system, the justification of the principle, and the truth of the principle. Thus, when the acceptance of the principle of truth connection explanation is justified, that is, defended by the system, the truth of the principle is explained and not a matter of luck.

The foregoing abstract explanation of how the truth of the principle of truth connection explanation can be defended in such a way that the truth of it is itself explained by the connection to the background system may be made more specific. It is capable of more precise formulation that has been the burden of my previous writing. I have argued that coherence must give a special place to certain general principles.[3] They include these two:

T. I am trustworthy in what I accept.
S. My trustworthiness in what I accept is successfully truth connected.

Now if I accept these principles and they are true, they would solve the problem of the truth connection and the coherence theory. They are needed as part of an acceptance system. They are supported by other components of a system recording past trustworthiness and successful truth connection. When we turn to the principles themselves, supposing that they cohere with the system, that is, are defensible on a fallibilisitc reading of them, then we can see that they contribute to the defense of themselves as they do to the defense of other claims. My acceptance of my trustworthiness in what I accept is defended by my trustworthiness in what I accept. The truth of my claim that I am trustworthy in what I accept is explained by my trustworthiness in what I accept. Similarly, and most fundamentally, my acceptance of the successful truth connection of what I accept is defended and explained by the successful truth connectedness of what I accept in a trustworthy way.

In conclusion, we find that the solution to the truth connection problem for coherence provides the solution to an antecedent problem. It is often argued against coherence theories that the coherence relation between internal states leaves open an infinite variety of alternative systems. If one thinks of coherence as a feature of the system, such as consistency or even consistency with some specified axiom system, then there will, in fact, be an infinity of coherent systems, and the solution of the truth connection problem will be hopeless. If, however, one construes coherence as a relationship between a target acceptance and a background system of acceptances, the problem of infinite variety and the problem of the truth connection have the same solution. The infinite variety of possibilities is constrained by the actuality of present acceptances of a person. Actuality constrains infinite possibility in the coherence theory. Moreover, the trustworthiness of what the person accepts and the successful truth connectedness of that trustworthiness provides the second constraint of actuality. There may be other possibilities of acceptance, of trustworthiness and successful truth connection, but that amounts to the mere truism that there are alternative ways of knowing. The appeal to the what is actually accepted by a person depends on the actual trustworthiness thereof and the actual success of the truth connection to yield knowledge. Coherence is a nexus of actual acceptances, trustworthiness and truth connection. Actuality trumps possibility to yield knowledge within the coherence theory.

There are other ways to solve the truth connection problem for a coherence theory. To present one way shows that the problem is not one of principle but only of detail. Moreover, and most happily, the answer shows the way in which coherence combined with truth may convert to knowledge. The conversion of coherence to knowledge can be the result of a truth connection explained by coherence and not just a matter of luck. Falliblism precludes any noncircular proof of the truth of what we accept. Coherence permits the explanation of the truth connection when we accept the truth. We have knowledge without proof that we have it. That is all we can have. It is enough to know and know that we know.

NOTES

[1] Lehrer (2000). For further critical discussion and defense of the coherence theory see, Bender (1989) and Olsson (2003).

[2] The theory I have defended is more complicated in that justification depends on acceptances, preferences over acceptances and reasonings concerning acceptances. For details, see Lehrer (2000).

[3] The principles are not intended as universal generalizations but, rather, as principles stating a general capacity of be trustworthy or successful in particular cases. My commitment to falliblism commits me to the assumption that the capacities are fallible in their application. Cf. Lehrer (2000).

REFERENCES

Bender, J. W. (ed.): 1989, *The Current State of the Coherence Theory: Critical Essays on the Epistemic Theories of Keith Lehrer and Laurence Bonjour, with Replies*, Kluwer Academic Publishers, Dordrecht.

Gettier, E. Jr: 1963, 'Is Justified True Belief Knowledge?', *Analysis* **23**, 121–123.

Lehrer, K.: 1965, 'Knowledge, Truth and Evidence', *Analysis* **25**, 168–175.

Lehrer, K.: 2000, *Theory of Knowledge* (2nd edn), Westview Press, Boulder and London

Olsson, E. J. (ed.): 2003, *The Epistemology of Keith Lehrer*, Kluwer Academic Publishers, Dordrecht.

Department of Philosophy
University of Arizona, Tucson
AZ, 85721-0027
USA
E-mail: lehrer@u.arizona.edu